PENGUIN BOOKS

BEYOND WAR

David Rohde is an investigative reporter for Reuters and a contributing editor for the *Atlantic*. A former foreign correspondent for the *New York Times* and the *Christian Science Monitor,* he is a two-time winner of the Pulitzer Prize and the author of *Endgame* and, with Kristen Mulvihill, *A Rope and a Prayer.* He lives in New York City.

D0104070

Beyond
WAR

REIMAGINING AMERICA'S
ROLE AND AMBITIONS
IN A NEW MIDDLE EAST

DAVID
ROHDE

PENGUIN BOOKS

PENGUIN BOOKS
Published by the Penguin Group
Penguin Group (USA) LLC
375 Hudson Street
New York, New York 10014

USA | Canada | UK | Ireland | Australia | New Zealand | India | South Africa | China
www.penguin.com
A Penguin Random House Company

First published in the United States of America by Viking Penguin,
a member of Penguin Group (USA) Inc., 2013

Published with a new introduction, chapter 8, and conclusion in Penguin Books 2014

THE LIBRARY OF CONGRESS HAS CATALOGED THE HARDCOVER EDITION AS FOLLOWS:
Rohde, David, 1967– author.
Beyond war : reimagining American influence in a new Middle East / David Rohde.
pages   cm
Includes bibliographical references and index.
ISBN 978-0-670-02644-9 (hc.)
ISBN 978-0-14-312511-2 (pbk.)
1. United States—Foreign economic relations—Middle East. 2. Middle East—
Foreign economic relations—United States. 3. United States—Relations—Middle
East. 4. Middle East—Relations—United States, I. Title.
HF1456.5.Z4M6287 2013
337.73056—dc23   2012039754

Printed in the United States of America
10 9 8 7 6 5 4 3 2 1

Set in Minion Pro with Chronicle
Interior and Map Designed by Daniel Lagin

To my wife and daughters

CONTENTS

CONTENTS

PART II
An Obama Doctrine?

AUTHOR'S NOTE

For personal reasons, I limited my travel while researching this book. In 2008, two Afghan journalists and I were kidnapped by the Taliban outside Kabul, taken to the tribal areas of Pakistan, and held captive there for seven months. Out of deference to the concerns of my family, I have not traveled to Afghanistan, Pakistan, Libya, or Egypt since the kidnapping. A list of the many journalists whose reporting, insights, and analysis from those countries this book relies on is in the acknowledgments, endnotes, and bibliography. I am enormously grateful to them for their intelligence, bravery, and outstanding work. Any and all mistakes, errors, and omissions in the pages that follow are wholly my own.

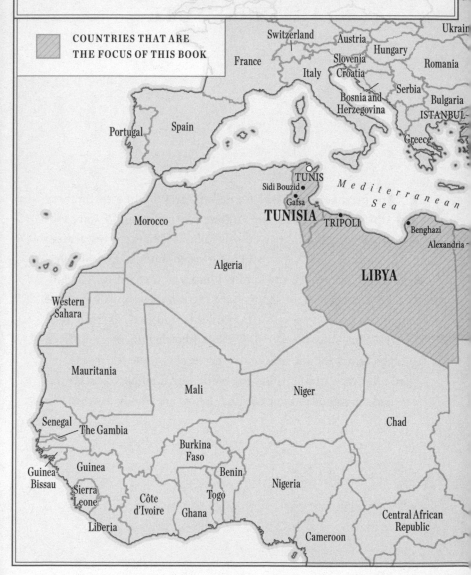

The Middle East, North Africa, and South Asia

COUNTRIES THAT ARE
THE FOCUS OF THIS BOOK

Switzerland
Austria
Hungary
France
Slovenia
Romania
Italy
Croatia
Bosnia and
Herzegovina
Serbia
Bulgaria
ISTANBUL
Greece

Portugal
Spain

*Mediterranean
Sea*

TUNIS
Sidi Bouzid
Gafsa
TUNISIA
TRIPOLI
Benghazi
Alexandria

Morocco

Algeria
LIBYA

Western
Sahara

Mauritania
Mali
Niger
Chad

Senegal
The Gambia
Burkina
Faso
Guinea
Bissau
Guinea
Benin
Nigeria
Sierra
Leone
Côte
d'Ivoire
Togo
Central African
Republic
Liberia
Ghana
Cameroon

Ukrain

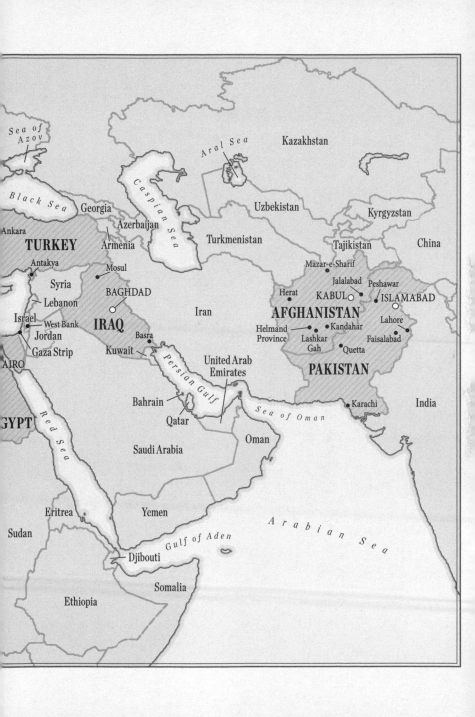

INTRODUCTION

When it comes to the Middle East, Americans have a clear and consistent message: Get out. Bring the troops home. Stop wasting our funds on fruitless efforts. Despite the sacrifice of sixty-seven hundred American lives and the spending of more than $1 trillion in Iraq and Afghanistan, the region seems as inimitably unstable, radicalized, and anti-American as ever.

This book is an attempt to find a new, more pragmatic, and more effective American approach to the Middle East. Numerous books have been written about American military and intelligence operations since 2001. This one examines the diplomatic, economic, and developmental efforts.

While covering Afghanistan, Pakistan, and, to a limited extent, Iraq for the *New York Times* from 2001 to 2009, I repeatedly embedded with American military units but found myself drawn to the American civilian effort over and over. Countering armed militants was a vital first step, but creating functioning local governments, economies, and schools, it seemed, was the key to long-term stability.

The same dynamic emerged when I reported in Turkey, Tunisia, Jordan, Israel, and the West Bank while working as a foreign affairs columnist for Reuters and the *Atlantic* between 2011 and 2013. Establishing basic security was crucial, but meeting public demand for growing economies, accountable governments, and individual rights was the core long-term challenge in the region.

The goal of this book is not to declare simplistically that there is a single doctrine or strategy the United States can adopt to instantly stabilize the Middle East. Nor is it to present an encyclopedic history of the region since 2001. What follows, instead, is a survey of various American nonmilitary efforts to counter militancy since 2001 and their results.

The book largely follows my reporting, which ranged from investigating obscure agriculture development programs in southern Afghanistan to the Bush and Obama administration counterterrorism strategies forged in Washington.

This book has three main goals: First, to highlight to Americans that moderates exist in the greater Middle East and to argue that they are an underutilized source of expertise, perspective, and ideas. Second, to examine the impact of the $67 billion the United States has spent in civilian aid in Afghanistan, Iraq, and Pakistan since 2001. And third, to draw initial conclusions about the effectiveness of those efforts, and in doing so to spark a debate about which ones to employ in the future.

Between 2001 and 2011, tens of thousands of Americans in Afghanistan and Iraq implemented a civilian effort designed to promote economic growth, build infrastructure, improve governance, strengthen government institutions, and expand education and health care. They also trained hundreds of thousands of local police, judges, politicians, journalists, and human rights advocates.

By almost any measure, those programs produced meager results. Washington squandered billions, largely neglected its true allies in the region, and failed to employ its most potent nonlethal tools: American expertise in technology, private investment, and education reform. Speed, visibility, and American political dynamics ruled. Patience, complexity, and deference to local cultures were shunned.

To an extent never seen before in American history, post-9/11 Washington relied on private contractors to achieve its foreign policy goals and waged for-profit war. At the peak of the wars in Iraq and Afghanistan, in 2010, 46,000 American contractors and 214,000 third-country and local contractors worked for the American government in both countries. At times, American government contractors outnumbered American troops.

Congressional investigators later concluded that the use of contractors minimized the number of American troops and hid the wars' human toll. Between 2001 and 2011, 8,560 U.S. soldiers and contractors died in Iraq and Afghanistan. Of the dead, 28 percent were contractors. Newspapers across the country faithfully printed the name of each American soldier who perished. There were no such commemorations of contractors.

At the same time, privatization proved to be wasteful. Investigators found that contracting was sometimes more costly than employing government workers, and tales of shoddy work abounded. All told, federal agencies paid a staggering $206 billion to contractors in Afghanistan and Iraq from 2001 to 2011. Investigators estimated that $31 to $60 billion was lost to waste, fraud, and abuse.

One clear lesson of the effort is that the United States should reduce its ambitions in the region. No American initiative, no matter how large, is a silver bullet in any region, country, or era, let alone one as complex as the early-twenty-first-century Middle East.

Another is that a more economic and less military-oriented effort will achieve more than the military interventions in Iraq and Afghanistan did. Of the more than $1 trillion the United States spent in Iraq and Afghanistan, 95 percent went to the American military effort. In some instances, drone strikes, covert operations, and lethal force may be necessary, but private investment, education, and normalized relations are equally vital weapons.

Intensive media coverage of anti-American protests distorts Americans' views of the region. The Arab world is not a monolith; nor are the world's 1.6 billion Muslims. Beneath seemingly chaotic events is a historic struggle between moderates and hard-liners, liberals and autocrats, pluralists and bigots for the future of the region. Its players are rationale actors. And its outcome will affect the United States, its allies, and the global economy for decades.

In public opinion surveys, clear majorities in Egypt, Tunisia, Turkey, and Pakistan called for democracy and personal freedoms— and Islam—in political life. The polling matched my experience in a dozen years of reporting. Arabs and South Asians said they did not want Americans to dictate to them. Nor did they want militants to impose an extreme version of Islam on them. Instead, they yearned for a third way, in which their countries could be both Muslim and modern.

Across the region, young people long for American high-tech investment, trade, and education. Public opinion surveys show an admiration for American technology, pop culture, democratic ideals, and ways of doing business. They also show a deep suspicion of America's intentions in the Middle East and its true commitment to democracy.

Twin imperatives should guide American policy. Terrorist groups should be targeted, but economic growth must be fostered as well. Today 60 percent of the Middle East's population is under the age of thirty. If they are to be gainfully employed, tens of millions of jobs will need to be created in the region by 2020, according to the International Monetary Fund.

In hindsight, Washington's civilian efforts exposed the dangerously weak state of its own civilian institutions. In the decades since the end of the cold war, the ability of the White House, State Department, and Congress to devise and carry out sophisticated political and development efforts overseas has withered. And while the complexity of global challenges has increased, rising partisanship and a twenty-four-hour news cycle in Washington have fueled demands for quick, inexpensive resolutions, which are illusory.

The use of contractors is a symptom—and a cause—of the decay in America's civilian foreign policy apparatus. The result on the ground has been a disjointed, wasteful, and largely failed civilian effort. In a volatile and rapidly changing region, there is a desperate need for a new American approach.

PART I

For-Profit War

CHAPTER 1

Little America

In the spring of 2004, a seventy-two-year-old American aid worker named Charles Grader told me a seemingly fantastical story. In a bleak stretch of Afghan desert that resembled the surface of Mars, several dozen families from states like Montana, Wisconsin, and California had lived in suburban tract homes with backyard barbecues. For thirty years during the cold war, the settlement served as the headquarters of a massive American project designed to wean Afghans from Soviet influence.

American engineers oversaw the largest development program in Afghanistan's history, constructing two huge earthen dams, 300 miles of irrigation canals, and 1,200 miles of gravel roads. All told, the project made 250,000 acres of desert bloom. The town, officially known as Lashkar Gah, was the new capital of Helmand province and an ultramodern world of workshops and offices. Afghans called it "Little America."

Intrigued, I hitched a ride to the town with Grader a few weeks later. A weathered New England blue blood, Grader was the last American to head the Kabul office of the U.S. Agency for International

Development before the 1979 Soviet invasion. In 2004, he was back in Afghanistan working as a contractor, refusing to retire just yet and trying, it seemed, to do good.

From the moment we arrived in Lashkar Gah, I was transfixed by Little America, its history and its meaning. At enormous cost, a sweeping American cold war effort had temporarily eased the destitution of one corner of Afghanistan but failed to achieve its loftier, long-term goals. Surveying the town, I desperately hoped America could do better now.

Instead, I would witness an epic tragedy that unfolded over the next eight years. Between 2001 and 2012, over nine hundred American and British troops died in Helmand—nearly twice as many as in any other Afghan province. At the same time, the U.S. and British governments spent billions of dollars in a desert province twice the size of Maryland with a population of only 1 million. Hundreds of highly paid foreign contractors arrived to train Afghan police, farmers, and government officials as well.

A clear pattern emerged in Helmand. When massive international efforts were made, real progress emerged. The provincial capital and other large towns in central Helmand grew more secure and thrived economically, and narcotics cultivation declined. But in isolated rural areas, poverty, corruption, and Islamic conservatism defied a scattershot approach.

On each trip, I met dozens of well-intentioned American and Afghan civilians trying to achieve those goals. But instead of triumphing, many of them ended up dejected, confused, and cynical. As American and British forces prepare to withdraw from Helmand in 2013, Afghans fear that the gains will crumble. The failures of Little America—and what they say about America's place, role, and future in the world—haunt me as well.

* * *

In 1946, Afghanistan's ambitious young king, Zahir Shah, hired a famed American heavy engineering firm, Morrison Knudsen, to build dams, irrigation canals, and a vast electrical grid across southern Afghanistan. At the time, palace coffers brimmed with profits from the sale of one of the country's few exports: Karakul fur from fat-tailed sheep. With European Karakul supplies cut off by World War II, the value of Afghan Karakul had soared, and with it, Afghan confidence.

Hubris filled the Boise, Idaho, headquarters of Morrison Knudsen as well. The firm embodied the growing industrial might and can-do ethos of post–World War II America. Its executives believed that the dams, canals, and roads they constructed around the globe continued the inevitable march of human progress. In 1954, *Time* magazine hailed the firm's cofounder Harry Morrison as "the man who has done more than anyone else to change the face of the earth." In the United States, the firm achieved its goals. In a forty-year span, it helped build the Hoover Dam, the Kennedy Space Center, and the Trans-Alaska Pipeline. But in Afghanistan, its project quickly went awry.

Afghan officials dismissed recommendations from Morrison Knudsen that the soil in Helmand be tested before constructing the irrigation canals. When water later flowed into desert fields, salt deposits in the soil killed crops. As costs spiraled, the Afghan government struggled to pay Morrison Knudsen. The high-stakes scheme flirted with collapse.

Fearing a loss of American prestige to the Soviet Union if the project failed, the U.S. Export-Import Bank began providing loans in the early 1950s. Eager to outdo the Soviets, American officials eventually promised to create an Afghanistan version of the Tennessee Valley Authority, the Depression-era hydroelectric system that spans five American states. The newly created Helmand Valley Authority would employ thousands of Afghan engineers and farmers and turn southern Afghanistan into the country's new breadbasket.

In the spring of 1960, the British historian Arnold J. Toynbee visited Helmand and discovered "a piece of America inserted into the Afghan landscape." Driving along miles of newly built canals, Toynbee felt as if he were traversing the southwestern United States, where American hubris seemed to have conquered nature. "The river that they are bleeding might be, not the Helmand, but the Colorado," Toynbee wrote in a memoir of his journey.

Laid out in a neat square grid, cold war Lashkar Gah was a sweltering, dust-covered town of fifteen thousand perched above the swirling brown waters of the Helmand River. Afghanistan's longest waterway, the Helmand sprouted green fields and orchards along its shores as it meandered through hundreds of miles of desert. The town had a four-lane, pine-tree-lined Main Street, a new hotel with a swimming pool and a tennis court, and southern Afghanistan's only coeducational high school. Downtown, a new movie theater played the latest Indian films. A few blocks away, American families ate hamburgers and watched Hollywood movies in a USAID guesthouse with a backyard cinema and patio.

The Americans prided themselves on being different from the British, but hints of colonialism emerged. Lucy Shook, a New Mexico housewife and devout Mormon, managed the USAID guesthouse in Lashkar Gah from 1965 to 1970. Young Afghan men wore bow ties, cooked food, and worked as servants. Shook called them "her boys." Educated Afghan engineers, doctors, and teachers from Kabul worked with the Americans on the project. Farmers, shopkeepers, and traders made up the remainder of the population.

The province and its massive development project even became the setting of a James Michener novel. After traveling through Afghanistan in the 1950s, Michener wrote *Caravans,* a 1963 yarn that described local Afghan disappointment with an expensive foreign aid project that failed to meet their expectations.

David Champagne, a Peace Corps worker from California who taught English in the local high school from 1968 to 1971, recalled a poor but peaceful community where Americans and Afghans alike never locked their doors. His wife, a fellow Peace Corps volunteer, worked as a nurse in the local hospital. They were "heady times," he later told me.

Champagne worked at an experimental school where Afghan and American teachers tried to infuse students—particularly girls—with a sense that they could achieve anything through hard work. Trying to combine "realism and optimism," he told young Afghans that long-term education and government reform could create prosperity.

In the end, the elaborate Afghan and American project irrigated only half of the acres promised. It consumed twice as much American and Afghan government funding as planned and took three times as long to complete. But its training programs produced hundreds of Afghan engineers and technicians with "American mindedness," according to Toynbee.

"Most of them have lived and worked and studied in the United States; some have married American wives," he wrote. "The new world that they are conjuring up out of the desert at the Helmand River's expense is to be an America-in-Asia."

Among the young Afghans who were transformed in the process was Fowzea Olomi. One of the first girls to attend the city's new coeducational school, she went on to become one of Helmand's first women to graduate from college. When I met her in 2004, Olomi remembered only a handful of words in English. But she could still tick off the names of her American teachers and recite verses of

"Twinkle, Twinkle, Little Star" and "Puff the Magic Dragon." After school, she played basketball with American children.

"It was a very good time," Olomi told me, eulogizing the functioning schools, clean streets, and tranquility of Lashkar Gah in the 1960s and 1970s. "I was very happy."

But her good fortune, like that of Lashkar Gah's, would be short-lived. Americans abandoned the city in the summer of 1979 as violence spread across the country just before the Soviet invasion. Twenty years of guerrilla and civil war ensued.

By the early 1990s, soldiers-turned-thieves roamed Lashkar Gah's streets, and warlords encouraged local farmers to grow opium poppies, the raw form of heroin. In 1994, residents welcomed the rise of the Taliban in Helmand's remote villages and applauded when thieves had their hands chopped off on a local soccer field. Crime plummeted.

For Olomi and other women, life fell apart. Her husband, who had gone to Russia to study medicine and resettled there, abandoned Olomi. In Lashkar Gah, Taliban religious police closed a girls' school she had opened to support herself. Olomi, who had chosen her husband at the age of twenty-five, watched helplessly as her daughter was forced by her husband's brothers to marry a cousin at thirteen.

Her hopes rose again in 2001, when American bombs drove the Taliban from power. Olomi dreamed of another American-backed renaissance.

"At that time, we really felt so happy," she said. "We felt that we were free now."

In June 2004, I drove into Lashkar Gah with Charles Grader and found a bustling town of a hundred thousand people filled with shops and open-air markets. The prosperity, though, was illusory.

The boom was largely fueled by Helmand's trade in opium poppy, the raw form of heroin, which had been spreading across the province since the fall of the Taliban. Throughout the trip, eight Afghan security guards hired by Grader's employer accompanied us for safety reasons.

In the center of town, the remains of Little America still stood. Afghans had erected eight-foot-high mud-brick walls around the one-story suburban tract homes the Americans had built during the cold war, a sign of differing Afghan and American notions of privacy. Rows of pine trees still lined some streets. And the headquarters of the Helmand Valley Authority—an impressive two-story office building—was in remarkably good shape. In some ways, Lashkar Gah reminded me of a small town in Texas, which bustled in the morning and grew still in stifling afternoon heat.

The province's governor, Sher Muhammad Akhundzada, was allegedly enmeshed in the opium trade, residents later told me, and enriching his own tribe at the expense of others. When I asked him about it, Akhundzada denied engaging in trafficking or victimizing other tribes. In the years to come, the drug trade and the corruption it spawned would act as a cancer in Helmand, creating dubious fortunes, deep inequality, and simmering anger at government corruption.

In a series of meetings with local officials during our 2004 trip, Grader promised to create public-works projects that would repair the province's American-built irrigation system, employ local farmers, and give them an alternative to poppy growing. As we crisscrossed the town that day, he defended the thirty-year cold war American project from critics who called it a costly boondoggle. Yes, the project had enormous cost overruns and failed to irrigate the acres promised, Grader said, but it trained thousands of Afghans.

"I feel so good about the education here," he said after meeting an Afghan engineer taught by Americans in the 1970s. "USAID trained a lot of people."

Grader was a marker of how the American approach to development had changed since the cold war. No longer a government worker, he was a private contractor paid $130,000 a year by Chemonics International, a for-profit consulting firm based in Washington. From Kabul, he managed a $130 million USAID contract to revitalize agriculture across southern Afghanistan and slow the exploding cultivation of opium poppy. The year before, Grader had spent six months in Iraq managing a $62 million USAID education reform contract for a Washington for-profit consulting firm named Creative Associates International.

Instead of USAID implementing projects itself, the agency doled out government aid money to private contractors, who then hired a cascading series of subcontractors to actually carry out the work. Chemonics was one of several dozen Washington-based contracting firms known as "Beltway bandits" established in response to the privatization of government services by the Reagan, Bush, and Clinton administrations. The owner of Chemonics, an Arizona businessman named Scott Spangler, worked at USAID as a political appointee during the George H. W. Bush administration. During the 1990s, he and his wife contributed $98,000 to political candidates, all Republicans. By 2004, 95 percent of the firm's $185 million in annual revenue came from USAID.

Under George W. Bush, the amount of money going to contractors rose by 70 percent. In theory, the use of contractors created competition between firms that saved taxpayers money, slowed the growth of the federal work force, and provided better services. Contractors could also be hired quickly, avoiding glacial federal government hiring procedures. And they could be let go as soon as a project was completed.

But Afghans loathed foreign contractors. They cited studies showing that 40 percent of foreign aid eventually returned to donor countries in the form of contractor profits. An Afghan engineer who worked for Grader said both Americans and Afghans were corrupt. Americans made their money through high overhead and expense rates, he said. Afghans made their money through old-fashioned kickbacks and bribes.

"For you, it's white-collar crime," he told me. "For us, it's blue-collar crime."

Lanky, with a thick shock of gray hair and a faded all-American look, Grader was an eclectic cold war throwback with renaissance flair. Perennially clad in brown bucks, he wore khaki pants and blue Brooks Brothers button-down shirts. The son of a postmaster and a housewife, he grew up in Marblehead, Massachusetts, a community north of Boston that the Graders had inhabited since the 1700s.

After graduating from high school, he went to sea as a sailor on a Liberian tanker. Later, he attended the Coast Guard Academy, earned a bachelor's degree from Boston University, studied at the London School of Economics, received a doctorate in economics from Tuft University's Fletcher School of Law and Diplomacy, and earned an MBA from the Massachusetts Institute of Technology.

His USAID career spanned the 1960s and 1970s, and Grader made his name as an advocate for reducing American staff at USAID missions and increasing the local staff. After retiring from USAID, Grader served as CEO of the world's largest bauxite mine in Guinea for five years, ran the senior executives program at MIT for a decade, and then returned to Afghanistan in 1996 as managing director of Afghanaid, a British NGO. His family had affectionately dubbed him "The Indiana Jones of Marblehead." A divorced father of two and lifelong vegetarian, Grader lived in a rented house in Kabul and spent his nights cooking cheese soufflés, listening to Italian opera, and reading Thucydides. He worried that America was in danger of following the path of ancient Athens, overextending itself and succumbing to Sparta.

Grader sometimes overextended in his own life. In 1997, he was nearly captured and killed by the Taliban while working with his Afghanaid team in northern Afghanistan. In 2003, airport customs officials arrested him in New Delhi after they found British colonial-era rifles from Afghanistan in his suitcase. Falsely accused of smuggling antiquities, he spent five weeks in a fetid Indian jail. When American diplomats came to visit Grader, they found him teaching microeconomics to other inmates.

After spending the night in Lashkar Gah, we made the long journey back to Kabul. During the drive, Grader grew pensive. American society had changed since the cold war, he told me. Companies were less loyal to workers. Government agencies were more politicized. Expediency was the norm.

"I'm frightened by what we're seeing," he told me. "I really feel the integrity is less."

Later I learned that Grader was right about USAID. The agency was a shell of its cold war self. Exaggerated accounts of American aid being poured down "foreign rat holes" prompted Congress to slash its budget. USAID's worldwide staff had shrunk from a high of seventeen thousand during the Vietnam War to three thousand in 2004. Following the 9/11 attacks, the agency's budget doubled, but it received virtually no additional staff to manage a torrent of spending. Overwhelmed USAID officials bundled contracts together, creating enormous contracts that could be implemented only by large contractors.

Grader said that when he ran USAID in Afghanistan in 1977, one hundred Americans managed roughly $250,000 in spending each. In 2004, sixty Americans managed roughly $80 million each.

Staffers struggled to design, put out to competitive bid, and monitor hurried and sprawling reconstruction projects.

For Grader and other USAID veterans, the post-2001 effort in Helmand was an anemic epilogue to an intrepid American cold war initiative. "Our policy is screwed up, and it's costing us dearly in time, treasure, and goodwill," he told me, warning that Afghans would quickly tire of foreigners. "It really bugs me how inept our government is operating."

At the time, I assumed Grader was exaggerating. Like generations before him, he saw youth as feckless and society in decline. Four months later, though, Chemonics fired Grader after only ten months on the job. Company officials said they could not comment on personnel decisions. Grader said he was forced out after he dared clash with USAID officials about the agency's programs.

Several months after visiting Little America with Grader, I returned to Helmand to learn more about the contractors leading the U.S. effort. My guide was a forty-year-old ex–U.S. Army paratrooper who asked to be identified by a pseudonym—Bob Williams—for safety reasons. Grader had hired Williams's small contracting firm as the subcontractor to carry out Chemonics' agricultural development work in Helmand.

An affable businessman with a soft spot for journalists, Williams agreed to give me a tour of his USAID-funded agricultural development projects in northern Helmand, one of the province's most dangerous areas. I was nervous. Williams relished the excitement.

As we sped across central Helmand's Dasht-e-Margo, or "Plain of Death," in a battered Toyota pickup truck, Williams casually chatted with me. Disdainful of the bulletproof vests worn by other contractors, Williams was dressed like a suburban American father on a Sunday afternoon. He wore baggy blue sweatpants, a loose white T-shirt, bright silver Nike sneakers, and a baseball cap from "Ritchie Bros. Auctioneers," a Fort Worth, Texas, firm that sold used construction equipment.

The vista outside our windshield was otherworldly. Instead of driving down a road, we followed a worn set of tire tracks across a gravel-strewn desert. The earth seemed eternally flat, with heat waves shimmering on the horizon. There were no trees, plants, or other signs of life. Everything was a variant of the color brown. Behind us, two of Williams's Afghan employees drove their own pickup truck as backup.

So much chalklike dust seeped into the cab that my ballpoint pen stopped working. After we crossed an asphalt road, Williams made a breathless announcement.

"We're north of the highway," he said. "This is bad guys' land."

As we continued driving, Williams's life story emerged. He was an American adventurer like Grader, but of a different generation. The son of a lawyer and a stenographer, Williams grew up on the East Coast. After serving in the army and graduating from his state university, he married his college girlfriend and moved overseas.

After the 9/11 attacks, business exploded. By the time I met him in 2004, he had a $4 million operating budget, fifty employees, and a dozen American government and United Nations contracts to build roads, repair irrigation canals, and teach farming across southern Afghanistan. He specialized in completing projects in areas where other contractors dared not tread. Taking risks, he found, paid handsomely.

"This whole security thing has become a convenient thing for people to hide behind," he told me. "I'm no braver than anybody else."

In truth, the agricultural development program Williams implemented for Chemonics and USAID was a shadow of the earlier, thirty-year American effort. In the 1970s, a dozen Afghan extension agents worked in each district. In 2004, USAID—via Williams— employed only two per district.

Using private contractors should have created competition for USAID contracts. Instead, Taliban attacks in southern Afghanistan prompted many firms to decline to work in the area. With few competitors, Williams garnered windfall profits despite having little experience.

Williams had his critics. Chemonics officials praised his firm's agricultural work but called his construction work shoddy. One Chemonics official told me a Thai engineer Williams hired to implement a $700,000 USAID project to construct nineteen small irrigation dams was incompetent, did not understand English, and submitted an initial design that was "a crappy little drawing." Westerners who worked for nonprofit groups called Williams a war profiteer and said he hired away their best Afghan engineers.

"We've just been reinforcing the predatory practices," the American director of one nonprofit told me, referring to corruption among Afghans. "If [Williams] is doing shoddy work and pockets the money, it absolutely reinforces the way the system works."

When I later asked Williams about the criticisms, he dismissed them and said he stood by his firm's work.

As we made our way farther north, I grew increasingly nervous. There were no foreign troops in the area. Following the fall of the Taliban, the only American forces to deploy to Helmand were several dozen Special Forces soldiers. They built a base in the center of the province in 2002, hired several hundred Afghan gunmen to protect them, and focused solely on hunting Taliban and al-Qaeda remnants.

As Williams and I drove, the first of roughly two hundred California National Guardsmen were arriving in Helmand to create a

"Provincial Reconstruction Team." In theory, the unit would bring security to Helmand and coordinate construction. In truth, their arrival raised the total number of American forces in the sprawling province to a mere 350, a fraction of the number needed.

In the late afternoon, we arrived at our destination: a camp built by American engineers when they constructed the Kajaki Dam in 1953. USAID had awarded Williams a contract to renovate and modernize the camp for workers from the Louis Berger Group, an American engineering conglomerate. Under another USAID contract, Louis Berger would repair the dam's two turbines, which had received no major maintenance since the 1970s, and install a third turbine. The repairs and expansion, it was hoped, would increase electrical output by 60 to 70 percent.

As we entered the engineering camp, I was astonished. It was as if a replica of a 1950s-era American motel had been built in the mountains of southern Afghanistan. A cluster of small one-story bungalows provided lodging. A large restaurant served American-style meals. A dilapidated tennis court provided recreation.

"We could fill that baby up," Williams said, referring to the bone-dry swimming pool. "If we could get this going, damn, it would be nice. This must have been so cool," he added. "I just want to make this nice."

Early the next morning, we made our way to the dam itself. As he drove, Williams sipped Crystal Light iced tea, his favorite drink. For a five-minute drive, twenty-four Afghan security guards in six pickup trucks accompanied us. They were from another contracting firm, United States Protection and Investigations, a start-up security company run by a husband and wife from Houston. Instead of deploying the soldiers to secure contractors, the United States hired more contractors.

The dam was an 887-foot-wide, 320-foot-tall wall of earth that held back the swirling waters of the Helmand River. Behind it, an emerald reservoir shimmered brilliantly in the sunlight. During the cold war, American and Afghan engineers rode paddleboats and picnicked here with their families.

We walked into the dam's powerhouse and found ourselves in a time capsule. The turbines, office furniture, and bathroom fixtures had all been manufactured in the United States and shipped en masse to Helmand. The Golden Gate Switchboard Company of Napa Valley, California, built the electrical panel. Westinghouse manufactured the turbines. A Youngstown, Ohio, firm produced the gym lockers in the men's room. The building was a shrine to a bygone era of American manufacturing might.

For the last twenty years, Afghan technicians had jerry-rigged the turbines and somehow kept power flowing. Events since 2001 had puzzled them. Eighteen different groups of American officials, contractors, and engineers had visited the dam since then, they told us. Yet the Afghans were still waiting for promised repairs to begin. Williams and I had no answers. We made small talk, praised the Afghans for their work, and took a few souvenir photos. After a thirty-minute visit, we left as well.

Struggling to contain a raging insurgency in Iraq, U.S. troops handed over security in Helmand to British forces in 2006. When I returned to Helmand in the summer of 2007, 5,000 British troops patrolled the province, a fifteen-fold increase over the 350 National Guardsmen the United States had deployed.

Despite the earlier efforts of Grader and USAID, poppy growth continued to spread. Poverty, instability, and an epic five-year drought made the crop a talisman. Six years after the fall of the Taliban, the province produced more heroin than any country on earth, including Mexico, Colombia, and Burma.

On a blistering August afternoon, I met Williams in his base of operations in a former USAID house in Lashkar Gah. Williams rented out rooms to contractors and journalists for fifty dollars a night. A dozen Filipino construction workers employed by Williams lived in trailers in the backyard where Americans had held parties and watched Hollywood movies during the cold war.

A hand-painted mural on the living room wall was a vestige of the house's former life. It showed Afghan merchants selling their wares in a bazaar outside Lashkar Gah near Qala-e-Bost, a famed arch built by the Ghaznavid Empire in the eleventh century. The artist had signed her name in neat, cursive letters: "Janet Howard," she wrote, "June 1968."

When the Taliban took over Lashkar Gah in the 1990s, they declared the mural blasphemous. Under their interpretation of Islam, any portrayal of the human form is forbidden. Using white paint, they blotted out every human figure.

That afternoon, I joined Williams in the living room as he met the brother and son of a truck driver recently killed by the Taliban. His firm had agreed to pay the man's family one year of his salary as compensation. With a translator at his side, Williams greeted the Afghans warmly and tried to console them.

"We just want to say that when somebody gets killed on a project, it is a big tragedy for us," Williams said. "Your brother, your father, he worked with us for some time, so I got to know him personally. He was a hardworking man and always ready for any task."

Williams praised the driver for several more minutes. Then he asked if there had been any progress in identifying the killers.

"Thank you for your wishes," the brother replied formally, displaying little emotion. "We have no information about these people."

"Are the police not interested?" Williams asked.

"The area is not under the control of the police," the brother explained. "So they cannot do anything."

"The only thing we want to do—and it's a small thing—is offer some compensation, which we will do," Williams said. "I wish we could do more."

"We are also deeply hurt by this," he added. "It also deeply affected our morale."

The brother sat silently. Williams looked at the son of the dead driver, a wiry young boy who appeared to be twelve years old. "How about the little one," he asked. "Is he going to school?"

"Yes, he is in the sixth grade," the brother replied, adding that the boy was the eldest of seven children. "The others are smaller."

After exchanging more pleasantries, Williams departed and a member of his staff handed the Afghans an envelope. The man and boy politely thanked him and departed. I later learned that Williams paid the boy fifteen hundred dollars for the life of his father, the same amount the Afghan government paid the families of civilians killed in American air strikes.

The following day, I met Rory Donohoe, the new USAID representative in Helmand. Donohoe was, in fact, an independent contractor. The agency was so short on personnel that it hired contractors to monitor its contractors.

A twenty-nine-year-old Californian, Donohoe had an MBA from Georgetown and brimmed with ambition. His age and limited experience reflected a reality of the post-9/11 effort. USAID and other civilian agencies struggled to get seasoned, midcareer professionals to take posts in Afghanistan. Some agency veterans had children and were unwilling to risk their lives. Others went to Iraq, which was seen as more of a potential career builder.

Tall, with dark hair and a boyish face, Donohoe told me he viewed the free market as the answer to Helmand's ills. To curb poppy cultivation, he and USAID's new director of agriculture in Afghanistan, Loren Stoddard, were proposing sweeping new projects that would create markets for the export of legal crops.

One afternoon, Donohoe and Stoddard gave me a tour of Lashkar Gah's former Soviet airbase. They excitedly described a $3 million plan to clear mines from the base and turn it into an industrial park and airport.

Standing a few feet from rusting Soviet fuel tanks and ambulances, Donohoe described how pomegranates, a delicacy in Helmand for centuries, would be flown to emerging markets in India and Dubai. Marble would be cut and polished for construction. And a forty-year-old state-run cotton gin would be privatized and expanded.

"This could be the commercial heart of southern Afghanistan," Donohoe told me.

A few days later, Donohoe and Stoddard showed me a project to teach Afghan farmers how to grow chili peppers on contract for a company in Dubai. Stoddard, a burly thirty-eight-year-old former food broker from Provo, Utah, said he had launched a similar project in Guatemala where farmers sold chili peppers to Walmart. A USAID subcontractor had brought three white Zimbabwean farmers, who had been driven from their farms by supporters of President Robert Mugabe to help show the Afghans how to grow the peppers.

"These kinds of partnerships with private companies are what we want here," Donohoe said. "We'll let the market drive it."

From the start, though, security problems plagued the chili pepper effort. After local villagers sneaked into the chili pepper demonstration farm and stole produce, USAID hired watchmen.

Twenty-four hours a day, seven days a week, two dozen Afghan men with assault rifles staffed six wooden guard towers that ringed the farm, safeguarding the chili peppers.

"Some people would say that security is so bad that you can't do anything," Donohoe told me, "but we do it."

Asadullah Wafa, the province's new Afghan governor, told me that the American reconstruction effort was too small and "low quality."

"There is a proverb in Afghanistan," he said. "By one flower we cannot mark spring."

As their presence grew, the British vastly expanded the small American base in Lashkar Gah and built a one-story building that contractors called "The Hilton." British government civilians lived in a modern dormitory bedecked with photos of Queen Elizabeth, Monet prints, and wide-screen televisions. Soldiers built volleyball courts, gardens, and bars.

"There were too many people who were in Helmand that were not in Helmand," a British contractor who asked not to be named later told me. "They couldn't see beyond the walls that protected them."

British and American civilian officials dismissed the criticism. They said they ventured into remote parts of the province for weeks at a time, were repeatedly attacked by the Taliban, and narrowly survived several suicide bombings.

At night, I attended surreal cookouts in fortified Lashkar Gah compounds inhabited by British, Dutch, and South African contractors. White Zimbabweans and South Africans grilled boerewors sausage and downed gallons of alcohol. To me, they embodied the mix of sincerity, greed, and absurdity that marked the post-2001 effort. Some were desperate for work. Others were desperate for adrenaline.

At times, I felt pity for contractors saddled with Sisyphean tasks. In 2005, DynCorp International, an American defense contractor the State Department hired to train Afghan police, sent two retired American deputy sheriffs to train Helmand's three thousand police. One was a California native who had trained police in the Balkans. The other hailed from a small town in Wyoming. Before arriving in Helmand, he had never been east of the Mississippi River.

At other times, I was baffled by the schemes USAID approved. In 2005, a USAID administrator brought eleven Bolivian cobblestone road builders to Helmand to teach their craft to local people. Afghans, who had driven on asphalt roads for thirty years, were uninterested.

In general, the most effective foreign organization was the generously funded American military. Marine and army units mounted sprawling campaigns to both kill Taliban and create jobs. Highly trained young officers and soldiers were generally impressive.

"The war is good for contractors, for journalists, for generals," I scribbled in my notebook during one visit, well aware that I too profited professionally from Helmand. "The war is not good for the Afghan people. How do we create 'The Good War' again?"

Between trips to Helmand, I looked at the American aid effort in other parts of the country. Across Afghanistan, contractors dominated.

Of the five major contracts issued by USAID in Afghanistan, only one—health care—was given to a nonprofit group. Louis Berger, the construction firm repairing the Kajaki Dam, received by far the largest, a $275 million contract to build roads, schools, and health clinics. DynCorp won a $164 million contract for training police. BearingPoint, the global management consulting firm formerly known as KPMG Peat Marwick, received a $41 million contract to reform the finance ministry and the economy. Management Systems International, a Washington, DC, consulting firm, won a $15 million contract to improve governance. And Creative Associates International, another Washington, DC, firm, won a $16 million contract to reform education. Other American companies won contracts to reform Afghanistan's defense ministry and help the CIA gather intelligence.

The Americans employed by the contractors ran America's political and cultural gamut. The head of DynCorp's operations in Afghanistan was a deeply religious and patriotic retired brigadier general from Arkansas who said blessings before every meal. Now in his midsixties, Herb Lloyd was one of only three Americans to rise from private to general in the United States military. While growing up in Hope, Arkansas, he knew Bill Clinton as a "chubby little guy" a few years behind him in school. Clinton went on to Georgetown. Lloyd went on to Vietnam. Wounded during two tours with a Vietnamese parachute battalion, he served a third, winning two Silver Stars, seven Bronze Stars, and two Purple Hearts. He later commanded troops in the United States, Germany, and Korea, and taught at West Point.

Since retiring from the military, Lloyd had worked for DynCorp administering American government–funded police training programs in Bosnia, Nigeria, East Timor, and now Afghanistan. Bearish, balding, and divorced, Lloyd exuded the energy of a man half his age and carried an M4 assault rifle wherever he went. He had narrowly survived a 2004 car bombing that killed four Americans and three Afghans just outside DynCorp's Kabul compound. He leaned Republican, spoke openly of his faith in God, and had an enormous desire to help the downtrodden. One of his proudest achievements was his "chickadee dees"—forty-eight young Bosnians he had helped win college scholarships to study in the United States on the condition that they return home to help rebuild their country afterward. All but one of them kept their word.

An unflinching believer in his country, culture, and company, Lloyd was convinced that the sheer power of the American example would transform Afghanistan's bedraggled and corruption-riddled police force.

"Our motives are selfless. Human beings can sense that," he told me. "They can pick it up right quick."

Lloyd vowed to stay in Afghanistan until "the job is finished" and the "very culture" of the Afghan police had changed. Americans had no choice but to succeed in Afghanistan, he said. Otherwise, terrorism would again threaten the United States.

"There is no option other than victory," he said. "Otherwise, America as we know it will cease to exist."

Phyllis Cox represented another side of America. A Harvard-educated lawyer and the daughter of famed Watergate prosecutor Archibald Cox, she was hired by Management Systems International to implement a USAID program to modernize Afghanistan's courts. Blue-eyed, with an angular face and short gray hair, Cox grew up in Cambridge, Massachusetts, attended Harvard as an undergraduate, and received a master's degree in international relations from Tufts University.

Shying away from politics and pedigree, she moved to Colorado, got married, had two daughters, got a law degree from the University of Denver, and built a thriving legal practice of her own. After a divorce, she signed up for a short-term legal reform project in Cambodia in 1994. Captivated by the work, she moved to Liberia, Guyana, and Bangladesh to run legal reform projects there. In 2004, Management Systems International hired her to administer USAID's legal reform project in Afghanistan.

In a country where 85 percent of disputes were still settled by tribal law, progress was painfully slow. Religious conservatives dominated the country's Supreme Court. While gradually enacting some reforms, they used patronage, corruption, and deeply conservative legal rulings to try to hold the country together.

When Management Systems International's contract ended in 2005, another Washington, DC–based contractor, Checchi and Company Consulting, hired Cox to run a USAID-funded rule of law program. When her mother's health deteriorated in 2006, she returned to the United States. After her mother's death, she worked in Cambodia, Guyana, Liberia, and Haiti before returning to Afghanistan from 2009 to 2011 for more legal reform.

"This place gets in your blood," she said. "You have to see the process in small increments."

Cox was right. Though press coverage of Afghanistan was overwhelmingly bleak, there were pockets of progress in the country. While most Afghan ministries were corrupt, reform efforts in three ministries succeeded. In 2002, the Ministry of Health set a clear goal after the fall of the Taliban to build rural clinics across Afghanistan that would provide basic health care. With funding from USAID, the World Bank, and European donors, it hired foreign NGOs to run the Afghan government's health programs in different parts of the country. In 2010, a series of studies commissioned by USAID showed dramatic improvement. After eight years of consistent effort, the average life expectancy of Afghans increased from forty-two to sixty-two, the maternal mortality rate declined by two-thirds, infant mortality dropped by a third, and the percentage of women receiving medical care during pregnancy rose from 16 per cent to 60 percent.

Critics pointed out that the survey was conducted in the safer parts of the country for security reasons, which skewed the results.

Still, the improvements—even if limited to more peaceful areas—were dramatic.

The Ministry of Rural Rehabilitation and Development took a similar approach. With funding from USAID, the World Bank, Japan, Canada, and Europe, the ministry created the National Solidarity Program, an Afghan-run $728 million initiative where twenty-nine thousand village councils across the country received small amounts of money to invest in the local project of their choice. Some villages built schools, others dug wells, and some constructed roads. Each village was responsible for maintaining and protecting its project after it was completed.

Afghanistan's third success story was the Ministry of Communications and Information Technology, which helped lead the country's explosive growth in mobile phone use. When the Taliban fell in 2001, Afghanistan's 30 million people had to leave the country to make a phone call. By 2012, 17 million Afghans—85 percent of the country's population—had access to mobile phones, and the sector accounted for 12 percent of Afghan government revenues. Across the country, 1 million Afghans were online. As many as a third of them used Facebook, according to one company's estimate.

Since 2002, the mobile phone sector had attracted more than $1.8 billion in investment from private investors, the World Bank, foreign donors, and the Afghan government. The cost of a SIM card dropped from $250 in 2003 to less than $1 in 2012. Along Afghanistan's highway network, more than sixteen hundred miles of fiber-optic cable had been dug, bringing affordable Internet access to Afghan homes for the first time. Internet service providers offered DSL packages in major cities. Other companies offered 3G and mobile GPRS connections.

In all three ministries, strong Afghan ministers crafted pragmatic, long-term strategies and patiently implemented them. Local involvement, realistic goals, and long-term commitments produced success. The question was how—or if—their success could be replicated.

In 2010, Little America became the epicenter of the Obama administration's troop surge. More than twenty-two thousand American marines—two hundred times the number of Americans deployed in 2001—arrived in the province. Roughly ten thousand British soldiers battled the Taliban as well.

Marjah, an obscure farming area outside Lashkar Gah built by American engineers in the 1960s, became the focus of a sweeping marine offensive. In 2010, the United States spent nearly $1.3 billion in the district, or $16,250 for each of its eighty thousand residents. The vast majority of the funding paid for American military operations.

Following the influx of thirty thousand foreign troops, security in Lashkar Gah and central Helmand vastly improved. The number of Americans assigned to training the Afghan army and police finally reached the levels American commanders had requested for years. The number of USAID officials in Helmand rose from one to eleven.

But a wave of Afghan civilian administrators promised by the government of Afghan President Hamid Karzai never appeared. Some effective local Afghan rulers emerged, but there were simply too few of them.

Donohoe, the young USAID contractor who oversaw other contractors in Helmand, became a USAID staffer, stayed in the province for three and a half years, and finally left Helmand in October 2010. Contractors complained about Donohue at times but respected him for spending so much time in the province. He was the longest-serving USAID field officer in Afghanistan. Most USAID officials—

and other civilians—rotated out of remote posts after twelve to eighteen months.

In a 2012 interview, Donohoe defended USAID's record in Helmand. He said only 1 percent of the agency's budget went to the cobblestone road and chili pepper projects. The agency completed the airport, doubled the electricity supply to Helmand, and reduced poppy production by roughly one-third. One of his biggest challenges, he said, was curbing an American tendency to do things themselves instead of relying on Afghans.

Eager to have concrete achievements during their one-year tours, American civilians and soldiers tended to implement projects themselves, Donohoe said. Afghan officials and firms often moved slowly and struggled with quality. By the time he left, he felt there had been a change in philosophy among U.S. officials.

"Everyone agreed that the only way for us to get out was for the Afghans to do things for themselves," Donohoe said. "The goal was to build an Afghan government that was capable of meeting the needs of its people."

During the cold war project in Helmand, he said, Afghans played a larger role in planning and decision making. And Donohoe found that the United States achieved more when it focused on a small number of modest goals over a longer period and worked closely with locals.

"Helmand is never going to be the Little America that was envisioned," he said. "But I do think Helmand is going to be okay."

If the United States continued to support Afghanistan, he added, the country would find its way.

"I think ultimately, the Afghans, they will figure this out," Donohoe told me. "They know what's going on better than we do."

Donohoe was right. Afghans often ran circles around Americans and other foreigners. But Karzai's failure to crack down on rampant corruption among Afghan officials proved disastrous. The greed of some contractors paled in comparison to that of many Afghan leaders.

Afghan governors appointed by Karzai profited from the drug trade in Helmand, seized land, and attacked rivals. With no strong institutions, merit system, or faith in the future, Afghans took whatever they could whenever they could for their families. Cynicism and graft ran rampant.

The idealistic Americans I came to know in Helmand met different fates. Grader, the cold warrior who served as my first guide in the province, never returned to Afghanistan. In 2010, he died in Marblehead after a brutal two-year battle with brain cancer.

Donohoe works for USAID in Peru. Lloyd returned to Arkansas. Cox moved back to Colorado. Williams, the contractor who took me to the dam, continues to work in Helmand. The Taliban or drug traffickers have killed seven of his Afghan employees since 2001.

In 2012, I met Williams in Washington. Under the Obama surge, business had initially boomed for him in Afghanistan. In 2011, Williams's firm had work in nineteen provinces. With U.S. forces preparing to leave, the number of provinces where he worked had now dwindled to seven. His company would never abandon Afghanistan, he vowed, and would continue to work there even if the Taliban took over.

The expansion of the Kajaki Dam that he spoke about so excitedly eight years earlier had still not been completed. In 2008, a five-day military operation involving two thousand British soldiers successfully moved a third turbine to the dam, and USAID hired a Chinese firm to install it. Yet Taliban attacks blocked the delivery of the nine hundred tons of cement needed to complete the job, and the Chinese firm abandoned the effort. Officials from USAID, which has spent $72 million on the stalled project since 2004, said work on the dam continues.

Missteps by contractors continue as well. A South African security guard who worked for the British government shot dead an Afghan colleague in 2009, was convicted of murder and sentenced to sixteen years in an Afghan prison. The *Washington Post* reported that former employees of Chemonics, which has received more than $430 million in USAID contracts since 2003, said their superiors kept their mouths shut about failing programs in order to keep contracts flowing. A spokeswoman for Chemonics said the company is now employee-owned and stands by its work in Afghanistan.

Louis Berger, the American engineering firm hired to repair the dam, paid a $65 million settlement after a whistle-blower exposed systematic overbilling of USAID. Company officials said the individuals involved were immediately fired, and the firm now has a new president, chief executive officer, and chief financial officer. And the husband and wife who ran the small Houston-based security firm that escorted us to the dam—USPI—pleaded guilty in 2009 to overbilling USAID by $3 million between 2004 and 2007.

U.S. troops stumbled as well. In January 2012, a video of four American marines urinating on the bodies of dead Taliban appeared on the Internet. Investigators later discovered it had been filmed in northern Helmand.

Williams loathed Karzai and other corrupt Afghans. But he also blamed American officials for failing to mount a serious effort until 2010 and instead relying on Afghan warlords to stabilize the country. In the process, they alienated the Afghan people.

"They see us coming and propping up these crooks," he said. "We do the same thing over and over."

Williams said he was ashamed of America's track record in Afghanistan.

"Our whole culture has changed since 2001," he told me. "What have we become?"

Looking back, Helmand acted as a mirror. Projects became more about Americans impressing their bosses back home than about creating lasting results on the ground for Afghans. American idealism—our great asset and flaw—faded. The name Little America took on a new meaning for me. It became a reference to a diminished America that had lost its way.

CHAPTER 2

Law and Disorder in Iraq

S ix weeks before American forces invaded Iraq in 2003, the Bush administration chose Jay Garner, a retired U.S. Army general, to be the American civilian administrator of post-Saddam Iraq. A blunt sixty-four-year-old Florida native who had led relief operations in northern Iraq after the first Gulf War, Garner began frantically pulling together a staff to manage a fractious nation the size of California.

Three weeks before the invasion, Garner met with National Security Adviser Condoleezza Rice and National Security Council officials to brief them on his plans. He and a team of experts from various civilian agencies said they believed a large contingent of American and European police officers would be needed to train a new Iraqi police force and prevent lawlessness. Garner unveiled an ambitious proposal to send five thousand American and foreign advisers to Iraq. Richard Mayer, a Justice Department police-training expert on his staff, had put together a detailed inch-and-a-half-thick plan that included organizational tables, budgets, and schedules.

The proposal was sweeping but not unprecedented. In Kosovo, a place one-tenth the size of Iraq, the United Nations had deployed forty-eight hundred foreign police officers to train locals and help deter crime. In Bosnia, two thousand international police officers had trained and monitored local forces.

In Mayer's analysis, two clear lessons had emerged from the Balkans. First, he believed that following a strategy he called "law and order first" was vital. If an effective police force and judicial system were not quickly created in Iraq, all other postwar reform and reconstruction efforts would stall. Second, Mayer believed that flooding local police stations with foreign trainers would help ensure that Iraqi police officers actually applied the training they received. The presence of foreigners also helped deter brutality, corruption, and infiltration by militias.

Garner and others on his staff warned administration officials that the Iraqi police, after decades of neglect and corruption, would collapse after the invasion. The police were "at the bottom of the security food chain," Garner recalled saying at the NSC meeting. "They didn't train. They didn't patrol."

Garner was not alone. In February, Robert M. Perito, a policing expert and a former official at the National Security Council and the State and Justice Departments, had made separately the same recommendation to Defense Department officials. Perito had called for six thousand American and foreign police officers to be dispatched across postwar Iraq.

But NSC officials reacted with skepticism to Garner's call for five thousand trainers. A vocal opponent was Frank Miller, the NSC official who would oversee the White House's effort to govern Iraq.

"He didn't think it was necessary," Garner said in a later interview. Rice, who was chairing the meeting, said the administration would revisit the issue after Saddam Hussein was removed from power. She then moved on to other issues.

"We settled for 'Don't make the decision not to do this yet,'" Garner recalled. "Let us get there and then make the decision on what was needed."

In truth, though, ideology was distorting administration policy. In a speech a month before the invasion, Defense Secretary Donald H. Rumsfeld said that international peacekeeping operations could create "a culture of dependence" and that a long-term foreign presence in a country "can be unnatural." In interviews, Miller and Douglas J. Feith, the Defense Department's undersecretary for policy, said their goal in post-Saddam Iraq was to minimize the American presence and empower Iraqis.

Feith insisted that his "strategic thought," as he later described it, was "that we are going to get into very big trouble in Iraq if we are viewed as our enemies would have us viewed, as imperialists, as heavy-handed and stealing their resources."

Rivalries and distrust between government agencies also skewed American prewar planning. Frank Miller, the skeptical NSC aide, said a CIA assessment led administration officials to believe that Iraq's police could maintain order. Doug Feith blamed the CIA report as well. He said agency analysts deemed Iraq's police professional, an appraisal that events proved "fundamentally wrong."

John E. McLaughlin, deputy CIA director from 2000 to 2004, said intelligence officials made it clear in prewar White House planning sessions that Iraq's police were troubled. He insisted that the CIA was not at fault.

"I left these meetings with a clear understanding that this police force was not one that we could rely on," McLaughlin said in a later interview. "I don't remember the agency, or intelligence more broadly, reassuring people about the police force."

Nine days before the invasion, President Bush rejected Garner's proposal and the recommendations of civilian experts. He approved guidelines that called for only a limited number of American police advisers. They would not have the power to enforce the law. That would be left to the Iraqi police.

Three weeks after American forces invaded Iraq, U.S. Army Lieutenant Colonel Robert Waltemeyer looked sternly at the thirty Iraqi community leaders gathered around him, put his hands on his hips, and read them the riot act. Forty-eight hours earlier, several hundred American Special Operations soldiers under Waltemeyer's command had driven Saddam Hussein's forces out of Mosul, the country's third-largest city and an ethnic and religious tinderbox.

"I came halfway around the world to protect your freedom," the frustrated colonel said. "You are the elder statesmen and wise men of this community and I need your help. We won the war and now need to win the peace."

Looting had erupted across the sprawling metropolis of 1.7 million people in northern Iraq, and unknown gunmen were firing on American forces. Waltemeyer—bald, stocky, and at times brusque— was trying to act like the new sheriff in town.

The local leaders, a cross section of Sunni Arabs, Kurds, Yazidis, and Assyrian Christians, listened politely to the American's speech but said nothing. As U.S. soldiers patrolled the streets in vehicles flying large American flags, some residents waved. Others spat at them.

In later conversations, local leaders and residents angrily complained that American forces had entered the city too slowly after Iraqi troops withdrew, and stood by as most ministries, colleges, and hospitals were looted. At the same time, clashes erupted between armed groups. Doctors said twenty-five to thirty people died in the first forty-eight hours of the American occupation. Over time, those numbers would spiral.

At the center of it all was Waltemeyer, a forty-two-year-old Special Forces colonel. From his base at the looted Mosul airport, Waltemeyer served as mayor, prosecutor, police chief, and public-works director in one. In public, he tried to convey the image of a take-no-prisoners strongman. In truth, he had only several hundred soldiers and no engineers, police, city managers, or other civilian experts to help him. Surrounded by an often hostile population, he and his troops were expected to somehow pacify and administer a city of dizzying ethnic and political complexity.

"Mosul has the promise to be a model community of a free democratic Iraq," he said at his first press conference. "But it ain't there yet."

As cities fell across Iraq, the same dynamic played out. Units of American troops rolled into towns and were confronted by angry locals who demanded that they police streets, repair downed electrical systems, and reopen schools. In Washington, Bush administration officials tried to play down the problem. Asked at a Pentagon press conference about the looting, Donald Rumsfeld gave an answer that became an infamous symbol of the administration's failure to properly prepare for governing post-Hussein Iraq.

"Freedom's untidy, and free people are free to make mistakes and commit crimes and do bad things," Rumsfeld said. "They're also free to live their lives and do wonderful things. And that's what's going to happen here."

It was also an example of an American tendency to focus on military force and ignore the vital role civilian efforts play. Military might alone is not enough to stabilize a country. Bush, Rumsfeld, and other senior officials ignored the warnings of career State Department officials, CIA analysts, and retired military officers that they would face chaos in Iraq. Instead, they were intent on quickly defeating Saddam Hussein's forces and avoiding Clinton administration–style "nation building." When they finally recognized that the United States had to mount a major effort to train Iraqi police, rebuild cities, and reopen schools, America's anemic civilian agencies were largely unable to carry it out. So were contractors.

In scores of communities across Iraq in the spring of 2003, scenes like the one I had witnessed in Mosul unfolded. Just as Garner's team had predicted, local police abandoned their posts en masse as government civil servants stopped coming to work across Iraq. Basic services disintegrated, and American military officers found themselves trying to repair municipal water systems and organize trash collection. Lawlessness, confusion, and uncertainty were rampant. In Baghdad, sixteen of twenty-three major government ministries were looted shells. Garner arrived with a team of twenty aides, toured the country, and tried to reassure Iraqis. But the postwar American plan to rule the country was in chaos.

After only three weeks on the job, Garner was fired by White House officials and replaced by L. Paul Bremer III, a former aide to Henry Kissinger. Bremer was even less prepared for Iraq than Garner. In a later interview, Bremer told me he had not participated in prewar planning and was never told of Garner's police training plan.

"I had only two weeks to get ready for the job," he recalled. "I don't remember being specifically briefed on the police."

When Bremer arrived in Baghdad on May 12, 2003, government offices were still burning. A full month after the fall of the city, looting continued. That night, Bremer gave his first speech to his staff.

"I put the very first priority on police and law and order," he recalled. "I said we should shoot the looters."

After Bremer's speech leaked to the press, American military officials promised him an additional four thousand military policemen in Baghdad. And a twenty-five-member Department of Justice assessment team arrived to draw up a plan to rebuild Iraq's police. They were daunted by what they found.

One team member, Gerald Burke, a fifty-seven-year-old retired Massachusetts State Police major, drove onto the grounds of the Baghdad police academy. Thousands of people—some, civilian crime victims in search of aid; others, police officers in search of orders—besieged a small group of American military policemen.

"We had people drive in with bodies lashed to the hood and lashed to the trunk," Burke recalled. "It was the only police facility that was open. People didn't know what to do."

The Justice Department team estimated that across the country 80 percent of Iraqi police had not returned to duty. Iraqis who had lived in a police state with virtually no street crime for twenty-five years were dismayed. They hailed Hussein's ouster but bitterly complained that the United States was not doing enough about spiraling crime.

In the face of soaring murder, kidnapping, and rape, Bush administration officials sent Bernard B. Kerik, the former New York City police commissioner, to Baghdad to lead the police training effort. Pentagon officials gave Kerik ten days to prepare for the job and little guidance.

With no experience in Iraq or overseas police training, Kerik said that one of the ways he prepared was by watching A&E documentaries on Saddam Hussein. He was never told of Garner's police training plan.

"Looking back, I really don't know what their plan was," Kerik said in a 2006 interview.

When Kerik arrived in Baghdad in mid-May, he found "nothing, absolutely nothing" in place. "Twelve guys on the ground plus me," he recalled. "That was the new Ministry of Interior."

Kerik put one member of his team in charge of training a four-thousand-officer unit to guard power plants and other utilities. A second aide was responsible for advising five hundred police commanders in Baghdad. A third was ordered to organize a border patrol for the entire country.

Kerik scrambled to reopen police academies and stations, screen thousands of Iraqis claiming to be policemen, and choose new police chiefs. Across Baghdad, American military policemen mounted joint patrols with Iraqis. All told, twenty-six hundred Americans tried to police a city of 7 million. New York, which has 8 million people, has thirty-four thousand police.

In rural areas, American military units launched their own impromptu police training programs that were completely separate from the civilian effort. Some lasted three weeks. Some lasted three days. Desperate for law and order, some American military officers declared local tribal leaders new police chiefs. In some cases, they welcomed repentant former supporters of Hussein back on the job.

Over the course of the summer of 2003, forty thousand Iraqi police officers returned to duty nationwide, and thirty-five police stations in Baghdad reopened. The numbers were promising but corruption was rampant. Insurgents and former criminals posed as policemen and infiltrated the force. And large parts of the population distrusted the former government officials Americans made police chiefs.

Fearing that long-term criminality and corruption would undermine any new Iraqi government, the twenty-five-member Justice Department assessment team drafted a plan to train a fifty-thousand- to eighty-thousand-member Iraqi police force. At first, members of the team suggested that Iraqi police recruits receive six months of training, the amount of time the trainers in Kosovo had settled on. Kerik said he "started laughing," and calculated that it would take nine years to train the force. The team reduced academy training to sixteen weeks, and eventually eight weeks. Later, a State Department audit found that some Iraqi recruits actually received the equivalent of four weeks of training.

"If you took all of the post–cold war conflicts from the 1990s and combined them together, it would not equal what you're up against in Iraq," recalled Carr Trevillian, the leader of the Justice Department team. "Even if it were a benign environment."

To make up for the shortened classes, Trevillian proposed a sweeping field-training program similar to the one Garner had outlined before the war. The team calculated that more than twenty thousand advisers would be needed to create the same ratio of police trainers to recruits in Iraq as existed in Kosovo. Deeming that figure unrealistic, they proposed embedding sixty-six hundred American and foreign trainers in police stations across the country to train Iraqis and, if necessary, enforce the law.

Officials from the State Department said they knew where to get the trainers: DynCorp. Like USAID, the State Department had gradually become dependent on the use of contractors over the course of a series of postwar interventions in the 1990s.

DynCorp's rise from a little-known Texas-based aviation mainte-nance company to an indispensable wing of the State Department began in 1994. On the eve of the American invasion of Haiti, offi-cials in an obscure State Department office known as the Bureau of International Narcotics and Law Enforcement Affairs, or INL, re-ceived an urgent request. The administration needed forty-five American police officers to help secure the Caribbean nation after

American forces toppled military dictator Raoul Cedras and rein-stalled President Jean-Bertrand Aristide.

INL officials contacted DynCorp, which already had a $30 mil-lion contract from the bureau to operate counternarcotics flights in Latin America. Impressed with the company's aviation work, INL awarded DynCorp a small contract to recruit, hire, and deploy the forty-five American police officers to Haiti. State Department offi-cials viewed the hiring of DynCorp as an interim measure; DynCorp saw it as a business opportunity.

"We always saw it as a growth area because of the conflicts in the world," Stephen Cannon, a former DynCorp executive, told me.

Cannon was right. Throughout the 1990s, the government money kept flowing. A few months after winning the police trainer contract, DynCorp won a contract from the Bureau of Diplomatic Security to guard American diplomats in Haiti. When the United States intervened in Bosnia in 1996 and Kosovo in 1999, more money followed. All told, the State Department issued more than $250 million in police training and diplomatic security contracts to DynCorp for work in Haiti, Bosnia, and Kosovo.

After the 9/11 attacks, DynCorp's government contracts ex-ploded. Between 2001 and 2011, the firm received $7.4 billion in contracts from the State Department and Pentagon in Afghanistan and Iraq. It became the third-largest American contractor in the two wars, behind only the massive oil and defense conglomerate Halliburton and a Kuwaiti-based firm, Agility, which provided food to American troops in Iraq.

While the Bush administration had largely ignored the need for po-lice in Iraq, DynCorp had banked on it. After the invasion, the com-pany posted help-wanted ads online and compiled a list of 1,150 active and retired American police officers who were interested in serving in Iraq. Under pressure for immediate results, the Justice Department team agreed that DynCorp should recruit the 6,600 trainers. On June 2, Bremer approved the plan.

The trainers, though, never materialized. Over the next six months, just fifty police advisers arrived in Iraq, even as the intensifying insurgency was presenting a much more lethal set of problems. Bremer, National Security Council staffers, and State Department officials all blamed one another for the problem.

"We and DynCorp were ready to go by June," a senior State Department official later told me. "But no money was provided for this purpose."

Miller, the National Security Council staffer who coordinated the postwar effort, said he was never told about the shortage of money. Miller said Bremer never made the need for field trainers a major issue. And DynCorp, meanwhile, waited.

"If at any point Bremer had said, 'I just saw a report and I need sixty-six hundred,' that would have made this a front-burner issue," Miller told me. "I don't recall that as an issue."

Bremer insisted that he pushed for more trainers throughout the summer of 2003. Over and over he was told that DynCorp was unable to find Americans and that no foreign countries were willing to send large numbers of police trainers.

"DynCorp was not producing anybody," Bremer said. "We were doing the best we could with what we had."

In interviews, DynCorp officials said they responded to all the requests they received from the government.

Frustrated by their inability to get enough manpower, Bremer and his staff cut the target number of trainers nearly in half, from 6,600 to 3,500. By September, they cut the number to 1,500. Finally, as 2003 came to a close, the State Department opened a sprawling training center in Jordan that would train 25,000 police recruits in the next twelve months. But once they went to their posts there would be few foreign field trainers to monitor them.

As the effort stumbled and shrank, no American officials publicly sounded the alarm about the situation. After spending only three and a half months in Iraq, Kerik returned to the United States. In early October, he praised the Iraqi police during a news conference with President Bush on the South Lawn of the White House.

"They have made tremendous progress," Kerik said. "The police are working."

Four years later, Kerik was indicted on federal tax evasion and fraud charges. He pleaded guilty and was sentenced to a four-year term in a federal prison in Maryland. The former leader of the American police training effort in Iraq was released from prison in May 2013.

After Kerik's departure from Iraq in the fall of 2003, infighting between American military and civilian officials involved in police training grew. American military officials announced that their training programs had produced fifty-four thousand police officers around the country. They said American soldiers would train another thirty thousand police in the next thirty days.

Civilian officials privately scoffed at the numbers. They believed that only superficial training programs could churn out so many graduates. Bremer said he repeatedly warned in NSC meetings chaired by Rice and attended by cabinet secretaries that the quality of police training was poor and focused on producing high numbers.

"They were just pulling kids off the streets and handing them badges and AK-47s," Bremer said.

Across Baghdad and the country, the spiraling insurgent attacks and lawlessness drove down popular support for the American-led occupation.

"We were the government of Iraq, and the most fundamental role of any government is law and order," Bremer said. "The fact that we didn't crack down on it from the very beginning had sent a message to the Iraqis and the insurgents that we were not prepared to enforce law and order."

Burke, the retired Massachusetts State Police major, said he was impressed by the eagerness of Iraqi police officers to build a professional new force but appalled by the American effort.

"We had such a golden opportunity in the first few months," he said. "These people were so willing. Even the Sunni policemen wanted change."

By January 2004, Bremer himself viewed the field training program as impractical. American military officials did not have enough troops to guard civilian trainers posted in isolated police stations, particularly in the volatile Sunni Triangle.

In a final capitulation, Bremer and his staff backed a plan to reduce the number of DynCorp field trainers by two-thirds, from fifteen hundred to five hundred. The remaining funds would be used to intensively train senior Iraqi police officials.

In Washington, Secretary of State Colin Powell and his deputy, Richard Armitage, fought the reduction. They argued that the police trainers could still operate in safer areas outside the Sunni Triangle. In March 2004, they lost the battle in Washington. The field training of a new Iraqi police force—at this point some ninety thousand officers—was left to five hundred DynCorp contractors.

When the DynCorp trainers fanned out across Iraq in 2004, they were disappointed and shocked by what they found. As one DynCorp trainer put it, they had hoped to be "part of an emerging democracy, part of history." Instead, they found themselves completely overwhelmed—and undermanned—for the task they faced.

As Garner's team had predicted, Iraqi recruits were generally motivated but their skills were rudimentary. In Saddam's Iraq, resources were showered on the intelligence services and army, which were seen as more loyal. DynCorp trainers had to instruct Iraqis on the most basic elements of policing, from designing crime report forms to carrying out traffic stops.

Reed Schmidt, a police chief from Atwater, Minnesota, said he was trying to teach the police in the southern city of Najaf his two-officer method for pulling a driver over when Iraqi officers said they preferred their own method. The Iraqis told him how two police pickup trucks with seven officers each surrounded the suspect's car with fourteen guns. Schmidt realized that if any of the Iraqi police opened fire they would shoot one another.

"Aren't you worried about hitting another officer?" he asked.

"Sometimes that happens," the Iraqis replied, according to Schmidt.

In northern Iraq, Ann Vernatt, a sheriff's investigator from Eastpointe, Michigan, said she and five other trainers checked on fifty-five stations each month. The hour-long visits left her impressed by the officers' motivation but dismayed by the bleak conditions.

"They had rusted Kalashnikovs, which they cleaned with gasoline. Most of their weapons did not work. And they got paid very little," she said. "They'd sell their bullets to feed their families."

Other DynCorp employees said their greatest frustration was simply having too many police officers to train.

Jon Villanova, a North Carolina deputy sheriff, said he was promoted by DynCorp to manage other trainers in southern Iraq four months into his yearlong stint. Under the original plan drawn up by the Justice Department team, he would have commanded a battalion of at least five hundred trainers. What he got instead was a squad of forty men to train twenty thousand Iraqi policemen in four provinces. Villanova said he couldn't dream of giving the Iraqis the one-on-one mentoring American police cadets typically receive. In the end, his team struggled to visit their stations once a month.

"That hurt," he said. "You need a lot of time to develop relationships and rapport so they trust you and are receptive to what you are trying to teach them."

David Dobrotka, the top civilian overseeing the DynCorp workers, said security concerns prompted him to stop hiring advisers once the number reached five hundred. Attacks were so frequent that some trainers were unable to leave their camps.

"Early in the mission, five hundred were too many," Dobrotka said. "Some were just sitting."

At the same time, there were only two government employees and one contractor in Baghdad monitoring the performance of all five hundred DynCorp advisers spread across the country. Government auditors later accused DynCorp employees of selling ammunition earmarked for the Iraqi police. And they found that DynCorp failed to install proper fraud controls and that a subcontractor it hired stole $600,000 worth of fuel in 2003.

Richard Cashon, a DynCorp vice president, defended the company's performance. The employees involved in the fuel theft were fired, and the company reimbursed the $600,000 the government lost. He said the firm's only responsibility was to provide high-quality contractors. The design, administration, and monitoring of the police training program were the responsibility of the State Department.

"We are not judged on the success or failure of the program as they established it," Cashon said. "We are judged on our ability to provide qualified personnel."

* * *

Even as the police training effort in Iraq stumbled, DynCorp won more and more government contracts. Government workers eventually started to refer to DynCorp and other contracting firms as "body shops." Whenever the government needed personnel to do anything, from interrogating prisoners to performing housekeeping on a base, DynCorp and other firms hired experts in the required field and offered them to the government for a fee. Between 2002 and 2012, DynCorp provided translators to American troops in Iraq and Afghanistan, maintained helicopters the United States provided to Pakistan, trained police in Afghanistan and Iraq for the State Department, and won multibillion-dollar Pentagon contracts to build, supply, and maintain American military bases worldwide. After Afghan President Hamid Karzai narrowly survived an assassination attempt in Kandahar in September 2002, the State Department hired DynCorp to protect him. Within months, State Department and Afghan officials began to complain that the Dyn-Corp guards were far too aggressive in their tactics. Their conduct alienated Afghan and European officials as well as Afghans. American officials evenutally stopped using DynCorp personnel to guard Karzai.

Investigators later found that so few firms were willing to work in Iraq and Afghanistan that DynCorp won some of its largest contracts with little competition. When DynCorp was not included in a final round of bidders for a new police training contract in 2009, the company filed a protest with the Government Accountability Office and won. Despite seven years of questionable performance, DynCorp won another police training contract worth up to $1 billion in December 2010.

In the end, DynCorp and other contractors had little responsibility for the actual outcome of U.S. government efforts but continued to profit enormously. Under DynCorp's "cost-plus" police training contracts, the company spent as much money as it deemed necessary to complete a project, and the government agreed to pay a set fee as a guaranteed profit.

In short, it was impossible for DynCorp to lose money.

A bipartisan panel Congress created in 2008—the Commission on Wartime Contracting in Iraq and Afghanistan—found that the cost-plus contracts created no incentive for contractors to reduce costs.

"Their company was not carrying any risk whatsoever," said Charles Tiefer, a member of the commission and a professor at the University of Baltimore School of Law. "They had the government's credit card in their pockets. It was guaranteed, a percent profit."

The spectacular returns caught the eye of traditional defense contractors and Wall Street. In 2003, Computer Sciences Corporation, a longtime defense contractor known by its acronym, CSC, purchased DynCorp for $914 million. Less than two years later, CSC split the company and sold its security and aviation divisions to Veritas Capital, a Wall Street venture capital firm, for $850 million. Two years later, Veritas took DynCorp public. And in 2010, Veritas sold DynCorp to a Wall Street private equity firm, Cerberus Capital Management, for $1 billion.

Officials from Veritas and Cerberus did not respond to interview requests. DynCorp officials said Cerberus had changed 90 percent of the firm's top management and improved performance. Former DynCorp employees told a different story. They said that midway through Veritas's six-year control of the company a new management team began cutting corners, reducing costs, and emphasizing profit over performance.

In truth, DynCorp's owners and executives took advantage of overwhelmed government agencies whose staffing had been cut by repeated administrations and congresses. High-priced contractors, it seemed, could solve any problem. In fact, they could not. But as the civilian American efforts in Iraq and Afghanistan faltered, the owners of DynCorp and other contracting firms grew rich.

The chairman of Veritas Capital, Robert B. McKeon, appears to be the American who made the single largest profit from the wars in Iraq and Afghanistan: $350 million from the purchase and sale of DynCorp. On September 10, 2012, McKeon committed suicide in his home in Darien, Connecticut, according to local police. A Veritas official who asked not to be named said the cause was personal and not work-related.

CHAPTER 3

A Civilian Surge

Two days after taking the oath of office in January 2009, Barack Obama made a series of decisions that signaled a sweeping departure from the Bush administration's conduct of the war on terror. He signed two executive orders, one barring the use of harsh interrogation techniques on detainees, and the other ordering the closure of the Guantánamo Bay detention center. In a carefully staged Oval Office ceremony, a dozen retired American military officers stood behind Obama as he signed the order shuttering Guantánamo.

An event on the same day, January 22, 2009, drew less attention but would also have an immediate impact on the way the new administration battled the Taliban and al-Qaeda. Richard C. Holbrooke was sworn in as the Obama administration's special envoy to Afghanistan and Pakistan. For eight years, Holbrooke and other Democrats had assailed the Bush administration's strategies in the region. They said Bush relied too heavily on military force; mounted a paltry, contractor-dominated development effort; and made no serious diplomatic effort. Now Holbrooke vowed to implement a robust civilian surge.

But for the veteran diplomat, the next two years would be the most frustrating period in a storied diplomatic career that began in Vietnam and spanned five presidencies. On December 13, 2010, Holbrooke died of a ruptured aorta. Friends said he had worked himself to death.

In numerous ways, Holbrooke corrected and expanded the tepid Bush administration civilian effort. The Obama administration increased civilian spending in Afghanistan by 50 percent, from $2.8 billion to $4.2 billion. The number of Americans deployed in the country nearly tripled, from 531 to approximately 1,300, with roughly 380 posted outside Kabul. Across the border in Pakistan, American civilian aid tripled to $1.5 billion a year and staffing doubled.

Holbrooke slowed the illicit flow of ammonium nitrate fertilizer—which insurgents used to make roadside bombs—from Pakistan to Afghanistan. He focused so intently on agriculture that Secretary of State Hillary Clinton dubbed him "Farmer Holbrooke." And he reversed the Bush administration policy of supporting the eradication of opium crops in southern Afghanistan. He and American military commanders believed the practice only increased support for the Taliban.

In an effort to reduce the role of contractors, he funneled more money through the Afghan government and tried to increase Afghan capacity to rule the country themselves. He personally reviewed every contract issued by the State Department and USAID in Afghanistan and Pakistan. For years, Holbrooke had been preparing for the job. In 2006, Holbrooke toured Afghanistan with a nephew who worked for the UN. Visiting a police training camp run by DynCorp in western Afghanistan, he was appalled by the quality of the Afghan police and DynCorp's operations.

Each day, DynCorp trainers drove nearly one hundred miles to the camp in large four-by-four trucks. Holbrooke warned the contractors that if they continued to follow the same daily routine they would be targeted. Six months later, four of the trainers died in a roadside bomb attack.

He also felt that the Americans were asking the Afghan police to carry out impossible tasks. At one point during the tour, Holbrooke and his nephew, Mathieu Lefevre, drove through the desert with American-trained Afghan counternarcotics police. Four policemen had one pickup truck to patrol hundreds of miles of desert.

"It was impossible with the current resources to interdict the drug flow," Lefevre recalled. "He realized that there is no way they can seal the border."

But distrust of Holbrooke and political realities quickly stymied many of his plans. In the American embassy in Kabul, Karl Eikenberry, the new ambassador and initially a Holbrooke ally, fiercely resisted any action by Holbrooke to encroach on what he saw as the embassy's authority. In Washington, USAID officials deeply resented his review of their contracts. And White House, USAID, and Kabul embassy officials all complained that contracts and dozens of other documents languished on Holbrooke's desk for months waiting for his approval.

After Holbrooke's death, the civilian surge was widely viewed in the administration and the region as a failure, doomed by a lack of local partners, infighting inside the administration, and mistakes made by Holbrooke.

Holbrooke's experience showed that the difficulties the United States encountered in Afghanistan and Pakistan went far beyond the liberal belief that the Bush administration had been incompetent. The countries' challenges were so complicated—and the degree of difficulty in solving them so high—that they would confound the Obama administration as well. And if Afghanistan and Pakistan were vexing, so was Washington. Steps that seemed simple on paper—such as decreasing the use of contractors—proved enormously difficult in the face of our own decayed and dysfunctional civilian agencies.

Holbrooke's first step at the State Department was to assemble a team of experts and aides. As he had throughout his career, he broke through bureaucratic protocol and hired people with little government experience.

On the night before his appointment was announced, he reached out to Vali Nasr, an Iranian American academic and expert on Pakistan. Three months later, on a shuttle flight from Washington to New York, he made an impromptu job offer to former UN official Rina Amiri, an Afghan American expert on Afghan politics.

He also hired from inside the government. After Steve Berk, an obscure U.S. Department of Agriculture official, sent Holbrooke an unsolicited e-mail detailing his experience working on agriculture in the country, Holbrooke made him a job offer. When Vikram Singh, a young aide to the undersecretary of defense for policy, Michèle Flournoy, impressed Holbrooke during a trip, he hired him as well.

While the offers may have seemed spontaneous, Holbrooke was trying to create a group that would limit bureaucratic infighting. When it was complete, his thirty-member team had ties to every government department and agency vital to the office's success: Defense, Treasury, Agriculture, Homeland Security, Justice, USAID, the FBI, and the Joint Staff, among others.

As he had been throughout his career, Holbrooke was aggressive, imperious, and domineering. The sixty-eight-year-old diplomat, best known for brokering the 1995 peace agreement that ended the war in Bosnia, was known as "the Bulldozer." But in his new post, he exhibited less of his famed abrasiveness, and encouraged, challenged, and supported his staff, according to former aides.

Over the years, Holbrooke appeared to have mellowed. He worked grueling hours and pushed his staff hard, but his advisers said they relished the experience. Comparing his office to an Internet start-up, they praised the veteran diplomat for keeping the organization as flat as possible. All staff members had access to Holbrooke, they said, and he encouraged frank and honest policy discussions.

Amiri, the expert on Afghan politics, said Holbrooke insisted that she typically present the local perspective on events, not the Washington view. "He looked at me to give the Afghan lens, not simply the objective lens," Amiri said. "How Afghans would see things on the ground."

In a September 2009 *New Yorker* profile, Holbrooke described his method as "a form of democratic centralism."

"You want open airing of views and opinions and suggestions upward," he said, "but once the policy's decided you want rigorous, disciplined implementation of it."

His heavy travel schedule prompted complaints that he was unfocused and disorganized. For Holbrooke, intricate foreign policy problems could be understood only in the field. As a result, he traveled to Afghanistan and Pakistan once every two months. Throughout his career, Holbrooke had been frustrated by Washington's glacial pace and bureaucratic myopia. In 2009, those forces seemed more powerful than ever.

Ruffling bureaucratic feathers he promoted staffers who thought and acted outside the Washington box. One of them was Shamila Chaudhary. In February 2009, Chaudhary briefed Holbrooke on Pakistan, and he was impressed by her knowledge of the country's politics. That night, the twenty-nine-year-old Pakistani American received a phone call telling her to join Holbrooke at a meeting with Clinton the following morning. The call stunned Chaudhary. A civil servant, she had never before been invited to such a high-level gathering.

In the meeting, Clinton and Holbrooke discussed the various political players in Pakistan. Clinton said the administration should engage Nawaz Sharif, the former prime minister of Pakistan, and asked if it was true that Sharif talked with the Taliban.

"I made a joke," Chaudhary recalled. "And said, 'Which Pakistani government hasn't talked to the Taliban?'"

Holbrooke gave Chaudhary a thumbs-up after the meeting, apparently happy she had pointed out the Pakistan government's close ties to the Taliban. She impressed Clinton as well. The following day, Chaudhary was told she was being promoted to the State Department Policy Planning Staff. In 2010, she was named director for Afghanistan and Pakistan at the National Security Council. Her career path was a sign of the times. Chaudhary's first job at the department was as a contractor.

The daughter of Pakistani immigrants, she had grown up in Toledo, Ohio, graduated from the University of Toledo in 1999, and moved to Washington to get a master's degree in international relations from American University.

"I had always wanted to work for the government," she recalled. "My family was able to come to the U.S. and have a good life here."

But Chaudhary struggled to find government work. She applied for internships in different government agencies, including the State Department and USAID, but had no luck. In 1999, she won a David L. Boren national security fellowship. Created by Boren, a former U.S. senator from Oklahoma, the fellowship is designed to increase American expertise in countries that received little attention during the cold war. Chaudhary used her fellowship to study in Pakistan, returned to Washington, and could still not land a government position.

Exasperated and desperate to do some type of government work, Chaudhary took a step she had tried to avoid. She applied for a position with a Washington-area contractor. Immediately, she was hired as an intern by the Academy for Educational Development, a DC-based nonprofit that implemented contracts from U.S. government agencies and other clients in 150 countries.

Quickly promoted to a job as a research analyst, Chaudhary found that there was not enough work to go around at AED, but the firm always managed to have enough money to throw huge holiday parties.

For four years, she worked for AED as it implemented various USAID-funded democracy and governance projects abroad. In 2004, she was finally hired by the State Department.

AED, meanwhile, rode the post-9/11 spending blitz, winning sixty-five USAID contracts worth roughly $650 million, including contracts to overhaul higher education in Afghanistan and carry out disaster relief, infrastructure development, education, and agricultural services in Pakistan.

Auditors discovered systematic fraud by the company in both countries. In 2011, AED agreed to pay back the government $5 million to $15 million and gave up all of its USAID contracts. While technically a nonprofit, AED paid its executives vast salaries. In 2007, its president, Stephen Moseley, was paid $879,530 in compensation.

From the beginning, Holbrooke saw negotiating with Taliban as a key part of his strategy in Afghanistan. But current and former administration intelligence officials flatly dismissed the idea. In

March 2009, Bruce Riedel—a former CIA official—submitted a review of American strategy in Afghanistan and Pakistan to President Obama. Riedel concluded that the Taliban was uninterested in negotiations and called for a "fully resourced counterinsurgency effort" to break the Taliban's momentum militarily. Privately, the American intelligence community presented an even harsher assessment. CIA officials told Obama that the unanimous and uncontested view of the American intelligence community was that the Taliban was closer than ever to al-Qaeda. They said peace talks would go nowhere.

Holbrooke questioned the CIA's findings and opposed the blanket dismissal of diplomacy. He did not believe that negotiations with the Taliban should be launched immediately, but was convinced that peace talks would eventually be needed to extricate American forces from the region. If the talks were to succeed, he argued, years of careful preparation would be needed.

"For him, the purpose of his office was to devise a grand diplomatic strategy to end this war," said Nasr, the former adviser to Holbrooke. "The problem was that there were no takers in the beginning."

First, he wanted to see the outcome of crucial August 2009 presidential elections in Afghanistan. Afghan President Hamid Karzai, or whoever beat him, would play a central role in any negotiations with the Taliban.

Holbrooke and other senior administration officials were skeptical of Karzai. At a February 2008 dinner in Kabul, Joe Biden grew so angry at the Afghan leader's repeated denials of corruption that the then senator threw down his napkin, told Karzai, "This dinner is over," and left the room.

A month later, in a March 2008 column for the *Washington Post,* Holbrooke criticized the Afghan leader for failing to arrest an infamous Afghan warlord, Abdul Rashid Dostum, after he attacked, brutalized, and nearly killed a rival commander in Kabul.

"The effect on Karzai's standing and reputation has been enormous," Holbrooke wrote. "Excuses were made, but none justified his open disregard for justice."

Obama, Biden, and other senior White House officials were determined to no longer "coddle" Karzai, as they believed the Bush administration had done. Soon after Obama took office, unnamed administration officials leaked stories saying Obama thought Karzai was unreliable and ineffective. James L. Jones, the national security adviser, eventually advised American officials to work around Karzai as much as possible and develop relationships with provincial governors. And in an even blunter signal, Obama canceled the weekly videoconferences that Bush had held with the Afghan leader.

Holbrooke, meanwhile, focused on Afghan presidential elections scheduled for August. He wanted serious candidates to run against Karzai before the outcome became a foregone conclusion. And he hoped for a large turnout to ensure that the results were credible.

"He rightly or wrongly bought into the idea that the election could be cathartic for Afghanistan," said Nasr. "That it would produce a better government."

But the Afghan leader enjoyed a roughly 70 percent approval rating among Afghans, twice the rate of his nearest political rival. Most important, Karzai still enjoyed strong support among his native Pashtuns, the country's largest ethnic group.

Holbrooke's advisers were split over Karzai. Critics of the Afghan leader said the United States should try to quietly force him out. Others argued that ruling Afghanistan was an impossible task and that removing Karzai was unwise. And still others believed that only one scenario could defeat the Afghan leader: the myriad groups opposed to Karzai had to unite behind a single opposition candidate who was a Pashtun. The Afghan opposition, though, remained deeply divided.

Holbrooke urged several prominent Afghan American Pashtuns to run for the presidency—including former U.S. ambassador to Afghanistan Zalmay Khalilizad. When word of the meetings had eventually gotten back to Karzai, the Afghan leader decided the Obama administration was trying to oust him. In truth, Obama and Secretary of State Clinton—as well as Holbrooke—endorsed a "level playing field" strategy in Afghanistan. American officials would support any candidate who wanted to run for president but did not try to rally support behind a single opposition leader.

The approach proved disastrous. Each opposition candidate claimed—and in some cases believed—he was Washington's chosen surrogate. In the end, thirty people ran for president, dividing the anti-Karzai vote.

"No one knew whom the United States was backing," said a former Holbrooke aide who had opposed the "level playing field" strategy. "The whole process was mucked up by a very confused U.S. approach to the elections." Altogether, the United States and its allies spent $400 million on the August 2009 elections.

Some of Holbrooke's aides would later admit that delaying the election for several months would have allowed the administration to develop a clearer strategy. The Obama White House was overwhelmed as it tried to pass a massive stimulus to bolster the free-falling American economy, enact sweeping health care reform, and close Guantánamo. Opposition from congressional Republicans also slowed the administration's ability to fill positions across the government.

In Kabul, meanwhile, conspiracy theories swirled. An American hand was thought to be behind every major development in the country. On election day, Karzai's supporters—convinced the United States was trying to oust him—engaged in widespread voter fraud. Cell phone camera videos showing Karzai supporters stamping ballot after ballot for the Afghan leader were broadcast worldwide.

The day after the election, Holbrooke and Eikenberry met with Karzai to discuss the race. When Holbrooke, the senior American envoy to the region, told Karzai that he had not won the required 50 percent of votes and a runoff was required, the Afghan leader angrily insisted that he had won more than 50 percent of the vote and no runoff was needed.

After the meeting, Karzai called the State Department operations center and demanded to speak with Obama or Clinton, according to former administration officials. Obama, on vacation in Martha's Vineyard, learned of the request and contacted Eikenberry. The two men agreed that neither Obama nor Clinton would speak to Karzai.

Two days later, Holbrooke, Eikenberry, and the American commander in Afghanistan, U.S. Lieutenant General Stanley McChrystal, had dinner with Karzai. Eikenberry explained that Obama and Clinton would not speak with the Afghan leader. Karzai viewed the move as hostile and evidence that the British and Americans were plotting against him.

Several days later, the BBC reported that an "explosive" confrontation and "dramatic bust-up" had occurred between Holbrooke and Karzai at the meetings. European officials who were sympathetic to Karzai and resented Holbrooke had leaked exaggerated accounts to the media. The story quickly went viral. Across Afghanistan and the Web, Holbrooke was portrayed as Karzai's American taskmaster. Subsequent stories speculated that Holbrooke was trying to force Karzai to accept an American-backed "CEO" to run the government.

Two weeks later, tensions flared again. Peter Galbraith, the deputy special representative of the UN mission in Kabul—and a Holbrooke ally—accused Kai Eide, a Norwegian diplomat and the head of the UN mission, of covering up Karzai's election fraud. Eide, in turn, accused Galbraith of promoting a plan to force Karzai from office.

Galbraith resigned in frustration, left Afghanistan, and later publicly accused Karzai of being a drug addict.

An incensed Karzai refused to receive Holbrooke, and Obama had to send Senator John Kerry, the head of the Senate Foreign Relations Committee, to Kabul to meet with him. After receiving direct appeals from Clinton and Kerry, Karzai agreed to a November runoff. Then his chief opponent dropped out of the race, declaring the election process fraudulent.

For Holbrooke and the new administration, the election was a debacle. Karzai had secured another five years in office and was convinced the Obama administration was his enemy.

"If you're going to put a gun to the king's head, you pull the trigger," a former State Department official later told me. "They tried to kill the king and failed."

On one level, the Obama administration had made the same mistake as the Bush administration. Disdainful of its predecessor, the Bush administration was determined to distance itself from Clinton-style "nation building." The Obama administration, in turn, was determined not to "coddle" Karzai, as they believed Bush had. In both administrations, partisanship skewed policy.

At the same time, Obama's aloofness and unwillingness to develop strong relationships with people outside his inner circle—from members of Congress to foreign leaders—handicapped the administration. Obama's and Clinton's refusal to take Karzai's phone call after the first round of the election was a mistake. In hindsight, Bush's policy of consistent contact with the Afghan leader created a stronger working relationship with Karzai. Whatever an administration thinks of a foreign leader in private, a respectful public relationship is always more productive, particularly in South Asia, a region where public loss of face is deeply humiliating.

Holbrooke had erred as well. "Holbrooke was extremely blunt with Karzai," said one former aide. "You cannot behave this way in Afghanistan. This is not the Balkans."

Others said he was simply following orders. In his meetings with Karzai after the election, he was obeying instructions from Washington to deliver a tough message to the Afghan president. In the months ahead, the White House would complicate Holbrooke's effort to mount a renewed civilian effort as well.

At the end of August, General Stanley McChrystal, the top American general in Afghanistan, presented to the White House his assessment of the American war effort. In a bold step, he called for a forty-thousand-soldier American surge to carry out the military's new counterinsurgency strategy. McChrystal also called for the United States to improve the performance of Afghan officials across the country and "prioritize responsive and accountable governance."

To Holbrooke , McChrystal's plan was reminiscent of Vietnam. Holbrooke's experience in Southeast Asia forty years earlier had left him skeptical of overly optimistic military assessments. The son of a doctor, Holbrooke's best friend while growing up in Scarsdale, New York, was David Rusk, son of the former secretary of state Dean Rusk. After graduating from Brown University in 1962, Holbrooke joined the Foreign Service, was sent to Vietnam, and worked as a USAID representative in a small village in the Mekong Delta.

Over the next six years, he held a series of jobs that gave him an extraordinary view of America in Vietnam. He worked as staff assistant to U.S. Ambassadors Maxwell Taylor and Henry Cabot Lodge. At the Johnson White House, Holbrooke wrote one volume of the Pentagon Papers, the secret history of U.S. involvement in the war. In 1968, he was part of the U.S. delegation to the opening of the Paris peace talks with North Vietnam. At a 2009 conference on Vietnam, Holbrooke delivered a critique of the war that many interpreted as a veiled criticism of U.S. policy in Afghanistan.

"We pursued a policy that would have denied Vietnam to the enemy only as long as our ground troops remained, but would not have left the Saigon government strong enough to survive on its own, he said. When we send our young men and women overseas to fight for their country, we must be sure they're really fighting for our vital national security interests."

In Holbrooke's view, a central mistake the Bush administration made in Afghanistan was relying too heavily on the military to achieve its goals. Vietnam had shown him how troop escalations could be seen as quick routes to victory in elusive conflicts.

Vietnam also left Holbrooke dubious of Washington's ability to properly plan, implement, and sustain a complex, long-term effort. Whatever challenges lay inside Afghanistan, getting the White House, Pentagon, CIA, State Department, and Congress to unite behind a multifaceted plan was next to impossible.

"One thing he definitely understood was the daunting complexity of Washington," said Nasr, Holbrooke's former aide. "He knew what the strength of the United States was. And he knew its weaknesses."

In a 1970 essay for *Foreign Policy* entitled "The Machine That Fails," a twenty-nine-year-old Holbrooke—who had just ended his work on Vietnam—warned of the cumbersome nature of the American foreign policy apparatus. He said multiple government agencies—as well as multiple bureaus within the State Department—pursued their own bureaucratic interests and projects.

"Over time, each agency has acquired certain 'pet projects' which its senior officials promote," Holbrooke wrote. "These are often carried out by one agency despite concern and even mid-level opposition from others."

Forty years later, the lack of coordination and cooperation between officials and agencies was even more acute, he told aides and friends. While American military commanders viewed the counterinsurgency strategy in Iraq as a model for Afghanistan, Holbrooke, Biden, and Eikenberry were deeply skeptical. They argued that internal political dynamics in Iraq—not the American surge—prompted the sharp reduction in bloodshed there.

The debate came to the fore during ten National Security Council meetings Obama held in the fall of 2009 to review American policy in Afghanistan and Pakistan. At the State Department, Holbrooke and his staff prepared for Clinton a confidential paper on negotiating with the Taliban. Given the Taliban's success on the battlefield in 2009, Holbrooke was skeptical about their willingness to make concessions, but he thought talks could be an option in the future.

"He wanted that to be well cooked," recalled a second former aide who asked not to be named. "He wanted to make sure it was ready before he presented it."

Instead of backing Holbrooke's call for negotiations, Clinton dismissed it. She discussed the issue in private meetings with Obama and Robert Gates, the secretary of defense, but never raised talks in the National Security Council meetings. In late October, she told Obama that she supported McChrystal's request for forty thousand troops. Holbrooke agreed that more military pressure needed to be placed on the Taliban, but believed a diplomatic initiative had to be launched as well.

"In Holbrooke's mind, military pressure was key to any political effort," said the second former senior aide. "The problem was increasing the military effort in the absence of a clear political strategy."

On December 1, 2009, Obama announced a thirty-thousand-soldier surge in Afghanistan but said it would end in eighteen months. Politically, the president tried to strike a middle ground. Increasing the U.S. military presence helped him fend off Republican attacks that he was weak on defense. At the same time, putting an eighteen-month deadline on the surge appealed to Obama's liberal, antiwar base.

In Afghanistan and Pakistan, the deadline played out badly. Many Afghans argued that it encouraged the Taliban. The deadline meant that insurgents did not have to fight or engage in serious negotiations. They had to simply wait out the surge.

In Afghanistan's presidential palace, though, the White House's decision was interpreted differently. White House officials hoped that a time-limited surge would pressure Karzai to improve his own performance. But Karzai dismissed the deadline as posturing and remained convinced that the United States wanted to keep troops in the region to counter Iran, China, and Russia. Holbrooke declined to comment publicly but was privately dismayed by the lack of a diplomatic strategy.

For civilian agencies, the biggest problem with the surge was its deadline. Obama's time limit demanded immediate results. In the fall of 2009, U.S. reconstruction spending ballooned to $4.1 billion. In Kabul, USAID officials outlined enormous new projects. More than $750 million was budgeted for increased electricity production. More than $300 million was to be spent in a single year in Helmand and Kandahar to revive local agriculture and reduce poppy cultivation—with another $450 million for future agricultural projects.

USAID budgeted another $600 million to improve municipal governments, $475 million nationwide to help reconstruct areas in the wake of counterinsurgency operations, and $225 million for clean water. Another $140 million went to an initiative to train Afghans to properly appraise land and avoid property disputes.

In Kabul, USAID officials carefully tracked their "burn rate"—how quickly they were spending the money. In mid-2010, USAID officials celebrated when the spending reached $340 million per month. The figure became a sign of progress and was mentioned repeatedly in internal meetings.

The vast spending alarmed USAID representatives in the field, but the short time frame of the surge intensified the pressure for fast, visible results. In Nawa district in Helmand, USAID spent $25 million in a single year. The sum astonished the agency's local representative at the time, Scott Dempsey. The twenty-six-year-old former marine reservist turned aid worker calculated that the agency spent $312.50 for each of the remote district's eighty thousand residents.

Like Grader and Donohoe before him, Dempsey thought that spending the money over a longer period of time would be more effective.

"If that money could have been spread out with a long-term commitment," Dempsey said, "we would have been able to achieve long-term stability for Nawa, rather than good press for DC."

A final element that thwarted the surge was American infighting. To Holbrooke's surprise, he found himself engulfed in some of the most vicious bureaucratic infighting of his professional life. He never formed a close relationship with Obama and was never able to get a one-on-one meeting with the president.

Fairly or unfairly, Holbrooke's prominence in some ways made his job more difficult. His rivals in the White House and the State Department looked for the slightest indication of his famed imperiousness. White House aides attacked him, and on several occasions, Clinton blocked their efforts to have Holbrooke removed from his job.

Press coverage—an element that had helped him in the past—complicated his efforts. Inside the White House, seemingly positive press coverage hurt Holbrooke's standing. Aides to the president viewed the lengthy *New Yorker* profile as proof of Holbrooke's insatiable ego.

James Jones, the national security adviser, and Douglas Lute, the NSC official charged with overseeing Afghanistan, eventually went to bureaucratic war with Holbrooke. They denied him access to military planes when they did not want him traveling to the region. They limited the number of aides he could take on trips. And they held key meetings when Holbrooke was out of town.

As part of the effort to undermine Holbrooke's authority, he was excluded from the 2010 trip Obama made to Afghanistan after announcing the troop surge. White House officials knew that it would signify to Afghans that Holbrooke was not a major player in the administration. White House officials even plotted to have Holbrooke excluded from a 2010 Oval Office meeting between Karzai and Obama.

Lute, a retired general and Bush administration holdover who coordinated the Afghan war effort at the NSC, prepared talking points that would have had the American president tell the Afghan leader that the aides in the room had his "utmost support," according to press reports. Holbrooke, of course, would not be present.

When Clinton heard about the meeting, she insisted that Holbrooke be included.

Friends of Holbrooke advised him to quit. Afghanistan was hopeless, they said, and he was wasting his time. Holbrooke insisted on staying. While he struggled in Afghanistan, he saw opportunity nearby.

CHAPTER 4

The Rise of the Drone

Three hundred miles to the west in Pakistan, Holbrooke was more effective. He stumbled at first but then made headway in a place few expected.

"He ended up having a much bigger impact in Pakistan," said Vali Nasr. "He wasn't competing with the military the way the military and the civilians do in Afghanistan. He [had] a grand strategy. He believed that we needed to stabilize the government and we needed to close the gap in trust that had developed for decades."

With fewer rival American officials and more room to maneuver, Holbrooke's frenetic, intensely personal style of diplomacy blossomed. After a series of early missteps, he formed close relationships with senior Pakistani civilian and military officials. And for a brief twelve-month period, he eased the deep distrust Pakistani officials felt toward the United States.

In Islamabad, he visited leaders every two to three months and held press conferences where he tried to address Pakistani concerns. When he was in New York, he barraged Pakistani officials with phone calls. In Washington, he took the Pakistani ambassador to the United States out for ice cream on Sundays.

The administration's first major initiative in Pakistan, though, went awry, illustrating another challenge American policy makers face: the U.S. Congress. Led by Senator John Kerry, Senator Richard Lugar, and Congressman Howard Berman, Congress passed a bill in October 2009 that tripled American civilian aid to Pakistan. But over the objections of Holbrooke and other senior administration officials, lawmakers put strict conditions on the aid. For Pakistan to receive it, the U.S. secretary of state had to certify every six months that the country's military was subordinate to its elected government. And the secretary also had to certify Pakistan was taking action against Taliban militants sheltering on its soil.

From the perspective of liberals in Washington, the bill was an effort to end a long history of American administrations—most recently that of George W. Bush—coddling the Pakistani military. Between 2001 and 2007, the United States provided Pakistan with roughly $10 billion in assistance. At least 70 percent of the funding went to the country's military.

At the same time, anger had simmered in Congress at growing evidence that Pakistan's military was sheltering Taliban militants they used as proxies in its fierce rivalry with India. The Pakistani army's policy of covertly supporting some militants appeared to be backfiring. To the alarm of Americans, members of the Taliban had turned against the Pakistani army and taken control of the scenic Swat Valley, which lies only one hundred miles northwest of Pakistan's capital. Members of Congress hoped the increased aid would show the United States' support for Pakistan's struggle against militancy, strengthen the civilian government of President Asif Ali Zardari, and signal to average Pakistanis that democracy, not the Taliban, created prosperity.

On paper, the bill was an attempt to create a more substantial and effective civilian aid program. But the Pakistani military deftly turned the conditions into an asset, not a threat. Pakistan's right-wing media—which has close ties to the military—declared the conditions an affront to Pakistan's sovereignty. Normally fractious opposition political parties issued a joint statement calling the conditions "humiliating." Instead of bolstering the civilian government of Pakistani President Zardari, the increased aid made Zardari look like an American stooge.

As the outcry in Pakistan grew, administration officials said they had asked Congress to remove the conditions from the bill but failed. Pakistanis simply did not believe them. As in other parts of the greater Middle East, the perception of the American government as a finely tuned, nefarious machine, not an unwieldy cacophony of viewpoints, was widespread in Pakistan. And the conditions reinforced a theme that existed in Afghanistan and Iraq as well. Measures that Americans considered well-meaning were seen as patronizing in the region. Americans focused obsessively on the power of Islamic extremism and often forgot that another force—nationalism—was even more powerful. If France had offered the United States $1.5 billion in aid with a list of conditions, Congress would have quickly rejected it.

As in Afghanistan, Holbrooke wanted to funnel as much American aid money as possible through the Pakistani government and increase its capacity. AID responded slowly, exasperating Holbrooke and his aides. He ordered USAID to immediately suspend its aid projects run by contractors and see if they could be administered by the state of Pakistan or local NGOs.

"AID is just slow, turgid, and bureaucratic, they cannot do the things we want," said a former aide of Holbrooke who spoke on condition of anonymity. "This frustrated Holbrooke to no end. Holbrooke would just light into them every week. 'Why are we not

doing big infrastructure?' 'Why are we not doing private investment?' 'Why are we not doing private sector development?'"

USAID officials and some American diplomats complained
that Holbrooke repeatedly shifted the focus of the American assistance, particularly in Pakistan. When the Taliban appeared strong,
USAID funding was directed to the border area of Pakistan, a Taliban stronghold. When the country's civilian government had a political crisis, USAID funds were redirected to areas that might
increase the government's popularity.

Officials at USAID said the government system was simply too
lumbering to carry out such rapid changes. Whenever projects were
changed, contracts had to be rescinded; contractors had to be fired;
and new plans, programs, and contracts had to be created. The frequent changes cost money and time.

Frustration grew so high that a senior economist at USAID
filed a dissent memo criticizing Holbrooke's review of contracts.
The economist, C. Stuart Callison, argued that Holbrooke's goals
were laudable but the Pakistani government and local NGOs lacked
the capacity to spend $1.5 billion a year responsibly. For such a
large program, U.S. contractors had to be used for an interim
period.

"On the one hand, [USAID] is expected to achieve high impact
counterinsurgency and broad-based economic development objectives as quickly as possible," Callison's memo said. "On the other
hand, it is asked to do this by working through national and local
government channels."

"These are all worthy goals," Callison continued. "However,
they are contradictory objectives without a reasonable period for the
latter."

By the end of 2009, American relations with Pakistan—and
Holbrooke's standing—had improved. In October 2009, Hillary

Clinton made her first trip to Pakistan as secretary of state. Mindful of the recent aid debacle and long-running Pakistani complaints against patronizing American officials, her office adopted a new approach.

After years of American diplomats holding brief, tightly scripted press conferences and taking few questions, Clinton answered questions from Pakistanis at public forums. She patiently listened to attacks on American foreign policy from students, editors, and others and tried to address their concerns. After the visit, Pakistanis praised her actions, which Holbrooke supported.

When epic floods engulfed Pakistan the following summer, Holbrooke personally coordinated American aid efforts. In many ways, it was Holbrooke at his best—overbearing, peripatetic, and passionate. From Islamabad, he drove the American government bureaucracy. He demanded that U.S. military helicopters be shifted from war fighting in Afghanistan to delivering relief supplies in Pakistan. He met with Pakistani officials and ordered USAID to respond to their requests quickly.

And he deftly managed the local media, not just the American media. On Pakistani television sets, American helicopters delivered food to stranded Pakistanis. In some cases, Holbrooke arrived in refugee camps before Pakistani officials did.

In many ways, Holbrooke's effort that summer in Pakistan showed how a revitalized civilian effort could achieve success. On a policy level, he focused on the practical. On a diplomatic level, he created respectful relationships with Pakistani officials. And on a public relations level, he improved the image of the United States.

In Pakistan and the United States, Holbrooke called for a more respectful long-term relationship between the two countries. Unlike his predecessors, he expressed interest in the long-term welfare of the Pakistani people. He stopped incessantly focusing on whether

Pakistan had responded to the latest U.S. demands in the war on terror.

Despite the duplicity of some Pakistani officials, he argued that a long-term approach was needed. Holbrooke was fully aware that the Pakistani military was still supporting the Afghan Taliban as proxies against India and that some Pakistani generals were lying to his face. In a conversation with Holbrooke in 2010, I asked him why the United States did not cut its $1 billion a year in military aid to the Pakistan army. He said cutting aid was "off the table" because it would only increase distrust of the United States.

"This cannot be a transactional relationship," he told me. "We have to create a long-term relationship."

Holbrooke's other major diplomatic effort in the region—negotiations with the Taliban—also quietly gained traction. Despite the objections of General David Petraeus and other American military commanders, the White House privately agreed in January 2010 that an Afghan-led reconciliation process with the Taliban should be part of the U.S. strategy in the region. Four months later, Obama and Clinton told Karzai during a May visit to Washington that the United States supported his negotiation efforts. And on November 28, 2010, American officials and Taliban representatives secretly met for the first time since 2001. With German and Qatari officials acting as mediators, they held introductory talks in a village outside Munich.

Two weeks later, Holbrooke died. Within months, short American time frames and Obama's embrace of the CIA and covert drone strikes would gut the civilian surge in both countries.

Six weeks after Holbrooke's death, Raymond Allen Davis, a thirty-five-year-old American, parked his white Honda Civic in front of an ATM machine in the busy eastern Pakistani city of Lahore. Stepping out of his car, Davis walked to the ATM, withdrew some cash, and got back into his car. Inside his vehicle was a Glock handgun, an infrared light, a portable telescope, GPS equipment, two cell phones, a satellite phone, dozens of bullets, multiple ATM and military ID cards, and a camera.

Several minutes later, Davis stopped at a traffic light and two Pakistani men on a motorcycle pulled up alongside his car. Both carried pistols. What happened next is disputed. According to Davis, one of the Pakistani men brandished a pistol. Fearing he was about to be robbed, Davis picked up his Glock and shot both men dead. Witnesses said Davis shot both men in the back, got out of his car, and tried to take pictures of the dead men with his cell phone. He also apparently called for help.

Moments after the shooting, a Toyota Land Cruiser with fake registration plates carrying American men sped out of the driveway of the house where Davis lived in Lahore. Roaring down the street, the Land Cruiser tried to reach Davis but got caught in a traffic jam. The driver jumped the median, drove into oncoming traffic, and collided head-on with a Pakistani man on a motorcycle, killing him.

The Land Cruiser fled the scene and sped toward the American consulate in Lahore. During the drive, the Americans hurled various objects out the window, according to Pakistani police. A baton, scissors, several batteries, gloves, a compass with a knife, a black mask, a piece of cloth bearing an American flag, and four magazines containing one hundred handgun bullets were later found on the road.

The Land Cruiser made it to the American consulate. But two Pakistani policemen apprehended Davis, who had tried to flee as well.

Pakistani officials jailed Davis, charged him with double murder, and demanded that American officials hand over for questioning the four men in the Land Cruiser. American officials said the four had already left the country. They insisted Davis was a security official at the American consulate in Lahore, was in Pakistan on a diplomatic visa, and enjoyed immunity from prosecution. Pakistani officials flatly disagreed.

Rumors swirled in the Pakistani press. Some reports said that Davis worked for Blackwater, whose shootings of civilians in Iraq had been reported and assailed in Pakistan. Some accounts said he worked for DynCorp, which had also won a contract from the State Department to provide security guards to the American embassy in Islamabad. Right-wing Pakistani commentators fumed on television about out-of-control American contractors killing innocent Pakistanis, Iraqis, and Afghans.

Three weeks after the shooting, the *Guardian* in London reported that Davis—who remained in jail—was a former American soldier working as a contractor for the CIA. The news confirmed conspiracy theories in Pakistan and the region about the sinister nature of all American activities abroad. The shortcomings of American contracting in Iraq and Afghanistan had now emerged in Pakistan as well.

In spectacular fashion, the Davis case brought to light the CIA's exploding and poorly monitored use of contractors. The CIA—one of the most generously funded agencies in the federal government—relied on contractors to an extent never seen before in its history. And, like other government agencies, it struggled to train and monitor contractors.

A 2010 investigation by the *Washington Post* found that roughly 30 percent of the people working for American intelligence agencies were contractors. Around the world, contractors played an enormous role.

"Private contractors working for the CIA have recruited spies in

Iraq, paid bribes for information in Afghanistan and protected CIA directors visiting world capitals," the *Post* reported. "Contractors have helped snatch a suspected extremist off the streets of Italy, interrogated detainees once held at secret prisons abroad and watched over defectors holed up in the Washington suburbs. At Langley headquarters, they analyze terrorist networks."

The *Post* found that in the aftermath of the 9/11 attacks the CIA had hired contractors as a way to quickly scale up the size of the organization. As elsewhere in the federal bureaucracy, hiring procedures were so byzantine that using contractors was the only way the CIA could rapidly increase its workforce.

Davis was not the first contractor to embarrass the agency. In 2006, a CIA contractor beat an Afghan detainee to death while questioning him in the northern province of Kandahar. The contractor, David Passaro, a former Army Ranger from Connecticut, was later tried in an American federal court and sentenced to eight years in prison.

In the world of espionage, Davis's actions were unforgivable. He had violated a core principle of spy craft—never draw attention to one's self. Officers in the CIA and other intelligence agencies are drilled over and over again to flee rather than get into a public confrontation.

After the *Guardian* disclosed Davis's work as a contractor, other news reports confirmed that Davis was part of a vast network of CIA personnel in Pakistan. Obama, skeptical of the American military surge in Afghanistan, had approved a clandestine surge in Pakistan.

When Barack Obama took office in 2009, "targeted killing" was a phrase rarely used in relation to his optimistic young presidency. The former constitutional law professor uttered the word *terror* only once in his inaugural address. Instead, he promised to use technology to "harness the sun and the winds and the soil to fuel our cars and run our factories."

Oddly, technology enabled Obama to become something few expected. In his first three and a half years in office, he approved more targeted killings—primarily through drone strikes—than any modern president. He also dramatically expanded the ability of the executive branch to secretly wage war. As the enormously costly military and civilian surges played out in Afghanistan, drones emerged as a comparatively cheap and politically risk-free alternative.

Between 2009 and 2013, Obama carried out at least 318 covert drone strikes, six times the 44 ordered by the Bush administration. After promising to make counterterrorism operations more transparent and rein in executive power, Obama has failed on both counts. His reliance on drones distorted American relations with Pakistan and other nations where they occurred, drove up anti-American sentiment, and created instability, not stability, over the long term.

After taking office in 2009, the new administration, just as it had done in Afghanistan, was eager to differentiate itself from the Bush White House in Pakistan. While speaking publicly of multilateralism, Obama adopted a get-tough, unilateral approach in Pakistan. He secretly authorized a stepped-up American intelligence effort, and the CIA vastly expanded its covert operations. At the same time, the agency was given more leeway in carrying out drone strikes in Pakistan's tribal areas.

The decision reflected Obama's personal belief and the influence of John Brennan, a former CIA official who was Obama's new senior counterterrorism adviser. To a far greater extent than the Bush White House, Obama and his top aides relied on the CIA for its analysis of Pakistan. As a result, preserving the agency's ability to carry out counterterrorism, or CT, operations in Pakistan became of paramount importance.

"The most important thing when it came to Pakistan was to be able to carry out drone strikes and nothing else," said Shamila Chaudhary, the young Pakistani American analyst who advised Holbrooke and Clinton and worked on the National Security Council. "The bilateral relationship was there solely to serve the CT approach."

Initially, the CIA was right. Increased drone strikes in the tribal areas eliminated senior al-Qaeda operatives in 2009. And in July 2010, Pakistanis working for the CIA pulled up behind a white Suzuki navigating the bustling city of Peshawar. The driver of the car was an elusive al Qaeda courier who was eventually tracked to a large compound in the city of Abbottabad. On May 2, 2011, American commandos killed Osama bin Laden there.

The American intelligence footprint, though, extended far beyond the hunt for Bin Laden. In the American embassy in Islamabad, CIA operatives and contractors outnumbered American diplomats and USAID workers. Davis was arrested in Lahore, a city where few people believed Bin Laden was hiding. At one point, the CIA tried to deploy dozens of operatives across Pakistan, according to Chaudhary. The agency also recruited large numbers of Pakistanis, including a doctor who pretended to be administering polio vaccines in Abbottabad in a failed effort to confirm that Bin Laden was hiding in the town. But the CIA's most controversial tactic was its stepped-up drone attacks.

Established by the Bush administration and Pakistani President Pervez Musharraf in 2004, the covert CIA drone program initially carried out only "personality" strikes against a preapproved list of senior al-Qaeda members. Pakistani officials were notified before many, but not all, attacks. Between 2004 and 2007, nine attacks were carried out in Pakistan, according to a compilation by the New America Foundation.

In 2008, the Bush administration authorized "signature" strikes in the tribal areas. Instead of basing attacks on intelligence regarding a specific "personality," CIA drone operators could carry out strikes based on the behavior of people on the ground. A drone strike could be launched if a group, for example, was seen crossing back and forth over the Afghanistan-Pakistan border. In its final year in office, the Bush administration carried out thirty-three drone strikes in total.

In 2009, under Obama, the total number of strikes nearly doubled to fifty-three. Former administration officials said the signature strikes, in particular, resulted in the killing of civilians. As the strikes escalated over the course of 2009, Pakistani public anger grew and the American ambassador in Pakistan, Anne W. Patterson, privately complained that she was not being consulted by the CIA before strikes were launched.

Dennis Blair, Obama's first director of national intelligence, also criticized the escalating number of strikes. Holbrooke privately proposed that control over drone strikes be shifted to the U.S. military, which would make them public, subject to strict legal reviews regarding the killing of civilians, and force the payment of compensation to the families of innocent victims. The CIA quickly killed the plan.

In 2010, the number of strikes more than doubled again, to 118. When Cameron Munter replaced Patterson as ambassador in Islamabad in October 2010, he objected even more vigorously to the attacks. On at least two occasions, CIA director Leon Panetta ignored Munter's protests and launched strikes in Pakistan. One occurred only hours after John Kerry, the head of the Senate Foreign Relations Committee, completed a visit to Islamabad.

After Davis's arrest in January 2011, the CIA paused drone strikes, apparently fearing for his safety. After weeks of public rancor, the CIA struck an agreement with Pakistan's intelligence service, the Directorate of Inter-Services Intelligence, or ISI. Pakistani intelligence operatives paid roughly $2.4 million to the families of Davis's three victims, and Davis was released on March 16. Nine month later, he was arrested in Colorado after getting into a fight with a man over a bagel shop parking spot.

The CIA—again over Munter's objections—immediately resumed drone strikes. The day after Davis was freed, the CIA carried out a signature drone strike that Pakistani officials said killed four Taliban fighters and thirty-eight civilians. Already incensed over the Davis case, Pakistan's army chief, General Ashfaq Parvez Kayani, issued an unusual public statement, saying a group of innocent civilians and local tribal elders had been "carelessly and callously targeted with complete disregard to human life."

U.S. intelligence officials dismissed the Pakistani complaints and insisted that twenty militants had perished. "There's every indication that this was a group of terrorists," one official said, "not a charity car wash in the Pakistani hinterlands."

Surprised by the vehemence of the official Pakistani reaction, the national security adviser, Tom Donilon, questioned whether the strikes were worthwhile. Critics inside and outside the U.S. government contended that a program that had begun as a carefully focused effort to kill senior al-Qaeda leaders had morphed into a bombing campaign against low-level Taliban fighters. Some outside analysts even argued that the administration had adopted a de facto "kill-not-capture" policy because it had been unable to close Guantánamo Bay and create a new detention system.

In April 2011, the director of Pakistan's intelligence service, Lieutenant General Ahmed Shuja Pasha, visited Washington in an effort to repair the relationship. Just after his visit, two more drone strikes occurred in the tribal areas, which Pasha took as a personal affront. In a rare concession, Panetta agreed to notify Pakistan's intelligence service before the United States carried out any strike that could kill more than twenty people.

In May 2011, after the Bin Laden raid sparked even greater anger in Pakistan, Donilon launched a White House review of how drone strikes were approved. During the review, though, the strikes continued. At the end of May, State Department officials were angered when Secretary of State Clinton's visit to Pakistan was followed by three missile strikes.

As Donilon's review progressed, an intense debate erupted inside the administration over the signature strikes. Admiral Mike Mullen, the chairman of the Joint Chiefs of Staff, believed they should be more selective. Gates warned that angry Pakistani officials could cut off supplies to U.S. troops in Afghanistan. Clinton warned that too many civilian casualties could strengthen opposition to Zardari.

The CIA countered that Taliban fighters were legitimate targets because they carried out cross-border attacks on U.S. forces. In June, Obama sided with the CIA. Panetta agreed that no drone strikes of any kind would be carried out when Pakistani officials visited Washington and that Clinton and Munter could object to proposed strikes. But Obama allowed the CIA director to retain final say.

Five months later, the administration faced the worst-case scenario that Mullen, Gates, and Clinton had tried to warn them about. In November, NATO airstrikes mistakenly killed twenty-four Pakistani soldiers on the Afghanistan-Pakistan border. A furious Kayani demanded an end to all U.S. drone strikes and blocked all NATO supplies to U.S. troops in Afghanistan from crossing

Pakistani territory. At the same time, popular opposition to Zardari soared.

After a nearly two-month lull that allowed militants to regroup, drone strikes resumed in the tribal areas in January 2012, but the frequency of the attacks slowed dramatically. As of November 2013, twenty-three had occurred, quarter the number carried out during the same period in 2010.

Congress grew concerned about the accuracy of the strikes, and staffers in Senate and House intelligence committees began holding monthly meetings with CIA officials to review the attacks. But even with the CIA under more scrutiny, the strikes continued. The agency had won the battle inside the Obama White House.

Among the Pakistani population, the strikes have played out disastrously. In a 2012 Pew Research Center poll, 97 percent of Pakistani respondents who knew about the attacks said American drone strikes were a "bad thing," and 74 percent of Pakistanis saw the United States as an enemy, a 14-percentage-point rise from 2008. Other reports suggested that most Pakistanis dismissed American claims that 90 percent of the people killed by drone strikes were militants. They believed 90 percent were civilians.

Administration officials defended the strikes, saying they were popular with Pakistanis who lived in the tribal areas and had tired of brutal Taliban rule. And they contended that Pakistani government officials—while publicly criticizing the attacks—agreed in private that they helped combat militancy. Making the strikes more transparent would reduce public anger in other parts of Pakistan, U.S. officials conceded. But they said that some elements of the Pakistani government continued to request that the strikes remain covert.

While drones have battered al-Qaeda, they have not helped to stabilize Pakistan. The country's economy is dismal. Its military continues to shelter Taliban fighters it sees as proxies to thwart Indian encroachment in Afghanistan. And the percentage of Pakistanis supporting the use of the Pakistani army to fight extremists in the tribal areas—the key to eradicating militancy—dropped from a 53 percent majority in 2009 to 32 percent in 2012. Pakistan is more unstable today than it was when Obama took office.

In the end, drones are no substitute for the difficult civilian effort of helping local moderates stabilize Pakistan and marginalize militants. Missile strikes that kill members of al-Qaeda and its affiliates do not strengthen economies, curb corruption, or improve government services.

David Barno, a retired lieutenant general who commanded U.S. forces in Afghanistan from 2003 to 2005, said hunting down senior terrorists over and over again is not a long-term solution.

"How do you get beyond this attrition warfare?" he asked. "I don't think we've answered that question yet."

In the State Department and in Pakistan, Holbrooke's civilian surge slowly unraveled after his death. Clinton approached a variety of seasoned American diplomats about taking over Holbrooke's position but they all declined. Afghanistan and Pakistan were seen as doomed, and a quick route to derailing one's career. As in Helmand, serving in the region was not perceived as a one's patriotic duty; it was a carefully calibrated career step. Veteran diplomats wanted to know how the American effort in Afghanistan and Pakistan could serve their interests, not how they could serve the American effort.

Three months after Holbrooke's death, Marc Grossman, a retired career State Department official, was named Holbrooke's replacement. An able diplomat, Grossman had served as U.S. ambassador to Turkey and under secretary of state for political affairs. While Holbrooke had literally worked himself to death, Grossman took ninety minutes off each day for lunch and a workout, according to his aides. And in a trait that pleased White House officials, he cut off all contract with the media, stayed "in his lane," and focused solely on his area of responsibility.

When U.S.-Pakistani relations plummeted after the killing of Bin Laden, Grossman lacked the relationships and the mandate to ease Pakistani concerns. While Holbrooke had spent two years courting, cajoling, and delivering on promises to Pakistani officials, Grossman was starting fresh. Before the Bin Laden raid, he had visited Pakistan only twice. Arriving in Islamabad the day after the raid on a prearranged trip, he could do little more than listen to bitter complaints from Pakistani officials that their sovereignty had been violated.

Later, officials in the Punjab, Pakistan's largest province, rejected all American assistance, forcing USAID to reprogram the spending of $200 million.

In Washington, the White House marginalized Grossman as it had Holbrooke. When Obama made a secret trip to Afghanistan in May 2012 to sign a strategic agreement between the two countries, Grossman was not told of the trip beforehand.

And like Holbrooke, Grossman grew frustrated with USAID. The agency struggled to spend the $1.5 billion per year in civilian aid mandated by the 2009 Kerry-Lugar-Berman bill. Aides to Grossman said that the original goal of the bill was to mount large, visible projects—such as hydroelectric dams, canals, or roads—that would demonstrate America's commitment to the Pakistani people.

"They didn't believe in them," a former Holbrooke aide said, referring to large infrastructure projects. "They don't like them and they can't do them."

Development experts at USAID repeatedly refused to implement such projects. The agency's philosophy had changed since the days of the sprawling Helmand project. Training government workers and teachers and reforming health care were seen as effective development programs. Building dams, roads, and electricity plants were seen as bad development. USAID had become so politicized that it failed to follow orders. The former aide to Holbrooke described the mentality:

"We joined AID to do good development work in Latin America and Africa," he said. "We don't want to be part of your dirty war on terrorism."

While the American aid effort stalled, Pakistani business owners clamored for something else: access to American markets, private investment, and technology. After the 9/11 attacks, a central demand of Pakistani executives was that the U.S. Congress lift long-running tariffs on Pakistani textiles. The businessmen said they wanted trade, not aid, according to Chaudhary, the Pakistani American former State Department and White House official.

For years, the Bush administration tried in vain to get members of Congress to lift tariffs that protected their states' dying textile industries. Textiles imported from Pakistan into the United States, it was hoped, would create jobs and help stabilize the region. But members of Congress from both parties rebuffed the Bush White House. When Holbrooke tried, he failed as well. The inability of both administrations to get congressional support baffled Pakistani moderates.

"The families that own businesses, they say that to me all the time," Chaudhary said. "'We don't understand. There are so many of us that are ready and willing and pro-American.'"

Monis Rahman, a Pakistani high-tech entrepreneur, is one example. In the summer of 2012, Rahman was profiled by journalist Elmira Bayrasli in a magazine piece for the *World Policy Journal*.

Her piece—and future book—explores the challenges entrepreneurs face in the developing world. Rahman's rise illustrates how globalization and technology are changing some corners of Pakistan.

A talented student and the son of a UN diplomat, Rahman graduated from the University of Wisconsin at Madison with an engineering degree. Hired by Intel in the 1990s, he moved to Silicon Valley and worked on a team that developed a computing breakthrough: the Itanium 64-bit microprocessor chip.

"It was my dream job," Rahman told Bayrasli. "But once I got there, I realized that Intel wasn't enough."

With billions being poured into dot-com start-ups all around him, Rahman decided to quit his job and move back to Pakistan. He was determined to try to create the "next big thing." For him, it was creating Naseeb.com, Pakistan's first matchmaking site.

Before leaving, Rahman asked friends in Silicon Valley for advice. He met with Reid Hoffman, the founder of LinkedIn, whose first start-up was an online dating service called SocialNet.

After talking with Rahman about how to make the site thrive, Hoffman asked if Rahman had found his start-up capital yet.

"I told him I didn't have the time," Rahman told Bayrasli.

Hoffman then picked up his phone and dialed a number.

"Joe? It's Reid," Rahman recalls Hoffman saying. "Listen, I'm with Monis Rahman, who's starting a SocialNet in Pakistan. I'm going in on it. I think you should too."

To Rahman's amazement, Hoffman had called Joe Krause, founder of Excite.com. Then he called Mark Pincus, who was working on Zynga at the time. The two men agreed to make $25,000 equity investments in Rahman's online dating service.

"Neither had seen any plans or PowerPoints on Naseeb.com," Rahman told Bayrasli.

He returned home elated but immediately encountered problems. When Rahman tried to find additional investors, he hit a brick wall. Despite the fact that international franchises like Pizza Hut, McDonald's, Kentucky Fried Chicken, and The Body Shop had proven enormously popular in Pakistan, investors were leery due to the country's instability.

"The main issue that we're seeing is we've got this huge perception challenge globally, and it is interfering with investments that are needed to fuel growth," Rahman told Bayrasli. "Many investors and businesses don't want to be linked in any way to what's happening here."

So Rahman started small. From a room in his parents' house in Lahore, he launched Naseeb.com in 2001. The space was so tight that when one of the eight staff had to use the bathroom, everyone had to stand up to get out of the way. Yet with only $150,000 in hand and expectations to succeed, Rahman didn't want to waste the equity investments he had raised before leaving Silicon Valley.

Nor did Rahman want to squander his connections there. He recognized that mentors and networks were critical to the life of any start-up. And both are scarce in Pakistan.

While there are established business families, there is no tradition of exchanging ideas or opening doors for others. There is no trust. Pakistani businesses fear that ideas and trade secrets will be stolen. With weak courts, there is little recourse. Rahman, though, was lucky. Unlike most Pakistani entrepreneurs, he knew he could find support in the Bay Area.

By mid-2005, Naseeb.com had grown to the point where Rahman had to expand his team. For that, he needed the best talent, so he put ads in the major newspapers. Then he realized that was the wrong way to reach people who want to work for an online start-up.

"I built a site to post my own vacancies," he explained.

It got so much traffic that he turned it into a paid site, Rozee.pk, with a client list of 3,200 employers and more than 100 million job postings. Today it's Rahman's core business. After again battling perceptions that Pakistan was unstable, he received investment from Draper Fisher Jurvetson, a Silicon Valley firm with experience investing in emerging economies.

Rahman told Bayrasli he was doing more than making money. He was helping his country.

"It's more than just a service." he said. "I'm not just building a product. I'm trying to make people's lives better."

Rahman was not alone. The Acumen Fund, a New York–based charity, also managed to find a way to help Pakistan's poorest. Founded by a former Chase Manhattan banker, the nonprofit follows what it calls a "third way" of development.

Jacqueline Novogratz, the fund's head, argued that charity alone wasn't the answer because it too often failed to create long-term, self-sustaining solutions. At the same time, the market alone failed as well. Business ignored the abject poor because they did not represent a potential profit source. Novogratz embraced a concept she called "patient capital," which involves long-term investments in risky enterprises run by local businesses and nonprofit groups.

In Pakistan, the fund invested $14.9 million in organizations providing slum dwellers with affordable, legal housing; microfinance groups that try to help the poor raise their incomes to the point where they can buy health insurance; a group that helps farmers boost their profits by investing in livestock and drip irrigation systems; and a company building community clean water systems in major cities. Each project included follow-up by the firm's Pakistani partners, which included leading universities and companies.

In many ways, Acumen's approach was the opposite of the congressionally mandated spending under Kerry-Lugar-Berman. As of

November 2013, roughly $2.5 billion of the $9 billion in foreign aid appropriated for Pakistan between 2009 and 2013 had been spent. After years of spending too little on the civilian effort in Pakistan, the administration tried to spend money too quickly.

Alicia Mollaun, an Australian researcher studying USAID programs in Pakistan, said Pakistanis perceive little impact from the American aid. "The Pakistanis say we don't know where it is going," she told me. "They say we don't know where it's being spent at all."

PART II

An Obama Doctrine?

CHAPTER 5

Where Islam and Democracy Meet, Uneasily

As the Obama administration effort in Afghanistan and Pakistan sputtered, the Arab Spring inspired and then alarmed Americans.

In an astonishing nine-month period in 2010 and 2011, street protests in Tunisia and Egypt and an armed rebellion in Libya forced the overthrow of three longtime Middle Eastern autocrats. Formerly all-powerful rulers in Yemen, Kuwait, Jordan, Oman, and Morocco made political concessions to the opposition as well.

In 2012, hard-line regimes fought back. Syrian President Bashar al-Assad's violent suppression of peaceful protests sparked a brutal civil war. The Sunni rulers of Bahrain crushed protests by the country's disenfranchised Shiite majority. And Saudi Arabia's ruling family tried to placate opponents with a multibillion-dollar increase in government benefits.

Finally, in the fall of 2012, instability spread to Turkey, a nation Bush and Obama administration officials viewed as a model for the region. After Turkey backed Syria's opposition, the two countries exchanged artillery fire. As tensions mounted, Turkish observers complained about American passivity.

"We are now at a very critical juncture," Melih Asik, a columnist for the centrist newspaper *Milliyet* wrote in October 2012. "We are not only facing Syria, but Iran, Iraq, Russia, and China are behind it as well. Behind us, we have nothing but the provocative stance and empty promises of the U.S."

After decades of being dismissed as "the sick man of Europe," Turkey's appeal to American officials soared in the 2000s. By 2012, Turkey boasted a faster-growing economy than any European nation and a 40-million-strong middle class, roughly 60 percent of its population. For Obama administration officials, Turkey seemingly represented an alternative to the Middle East's three failed models of government: secular Arab dictatorship, authoritarian Islam, and American invasion. But Turkey's leader, Prime Minister Recep Tayyip Erdogan, displayed an increasing authoritarian streak.

Since taking office in 2002, Erdogan had overseen a near tripling of per capita income in Turkey; broken the Turkish military's decades-long grip on power; and declared that Islam, democracy, and capitalism were compatible. As part of Turkey's effort to join the European Union (EU), the conservative Islamist politician opened up the country's economy, overhauled its judiciary, and granted rights to women and minorities. He also completed a harsh International Monetary Fund loan and reform program and attracted massive investments from European and American corporations.

Erdogan also displayed a growing intolerance for dissent. In recent years, Turkish prosecutors have jailed more than seven hundred people and accused them of plotting coups that would restore the military to power. Generals, members of parliament, owners of television stations, university officials, and journalists have all been arrested in what appears to be a campaign to silence dissent.

Critics of Erdogan—who was imprisoned for four months in 1999—say he is exacting revenge on those who oppressed him and his party in the past. In the spring of 2013, Erdogan's response to protests in Istanbul's Taksim Square polarized Turkish politics. After the Turkish leader crushed the demonstrations by force, he badly damaged the country's image as a potential example for the region.

Desperate for an ally—and a model—in the region, the Obama administration stayed largely silent about Erdogan's excesses. On one level, Turkey shows how free-market reforms, consumerism, and technological change can help transform a Middle Eastern country. On another, it shows how slow moving political reform in the region can be.

Culturally, Turkey has an impact in the region that the United States and other Western nations can never equal. One example is Turkish soap operas. Broadcast across the Middle East, they have taken the region by storm, empowering moderates and enraging conservatives.

Each week, in a state-of-the art Istanbul television studio, the Islamic world's version of America's culture war plays out in a television series called *Magnificent Century*. A dashing Turkish actor plays Suleiman the Magnificent, the Ottoman ruler who conquered vast swaths of the Middle East and Europe, granted basic rights to Christians and Jews, and promoted education, science, and art. Early episodes of the program portrayed a young Suleiman cavorting with scantily clad women in the palace harem and drinking wine. The sex was frequent.

After the show's January 2011 debut, Erdogan, along with a number of other Turkish conservatives, complained that it ma ligned a revered ruler known as "the lawgiver" whose military prowess and legal reforms placed the Ottomans at the zenith of their power. Erdogan called the series "an attempt to insult our past, to treat our history with disrespect and an effort to show our history in a negative light to the younger generations."

Critics hurled eggs at billboards advertising the program, protested outside the television station airing the show, and filed more than seventy thousand complaints with the Turkish government television agency. In response, the show's producers shortened kissing scenes and toned down other prurient elements.

In interviews, the show's producers defended the soap opera, saying it contained other themes. Its dominant character was a woman, the Ukrainian slave-turned-concubine who eventually became Suleiman's queen. And the story line showed members of different faiths coexisting.

Halit Ergenc, the actor who plays Suleiman, boasted in an interview in the spring of 2012 about the show's religious tolerance. "This is the most important thing of the Ottoman Empire that allowed one family to rule for centuries," he said. "Sharing the same land with different cultures and different religions and respecting their rights."

As of the fall of 2013, *Magnificent Century* was airing in forty-five countries and was one of the most popular shows in the Middle East. It was the latest of a series of Turkish television soap operas to find a huge audience there.

What may someday be known as the Islamic world's cultural revolution began in 2006. A Saudi-owned Arabic-language satellite television channel, MBC, bought the rights to an obscure Turkish soap opera named after its heroine, Gumus—"silver" in Turkish. In a classic rags-to-riches story, the series recounted the struggles of an impoverished young woman who marries into a wealthy family. Dubbed into colloquial Arabic, censored of its raciest scenes, and renamed *Noor*—"moon" in Arabic—the series was a phenomenal hit across the Middle East.

Unlike Western soap operas, it focused on an extended family, a strong tradition in Turkey and the region. In 2008, the show's final episode drew an estimated 85 million viewers over the age of fifteen, according to MBC. The audience included an estimated 50 million women, a figure that represented more than half the adult women in the Arab world.

Like *Magnificent Century, Noor* violated conservative cultural norms. Some Muslim characters drank wine with dinner and engaged in premarital sex. One character had an abortion. And in a subtle twist, the lead male character, Muhannad, was the show's moderate and modern hero.

A loving, attentive, and loyal husband, he supported his wife's career as a fashion designer and treated her as an equal. Their successful marriage—which combined traditional loyalty and modern independence—was both popular, particularly among women, and groundbreaking. Some Arabic-language newspapers reported that arguments and even divorces occurred in several countries as a result.

Turkish academics believe the programs have subtly changed cultural norms in the Middle East.

"Somehow, in those serials, you have a very balanced adjustment," Aydin Ugur, a professor of sociology at Istanbul Bilgi University, told me in an interview. "Women are modern, but they are not degenerate."

In Saudi Arabia, conservative Islamic clerics denounced *Noor*. They declared the show "wicked and evil" and a "secular Turkish assault on Saudi society." They forbade people from watching the program or attending prayer services in T ohirts that depicted the show's two stars. The head of a Saudi religious council said the owner of MBC should be tried and potentially executed for airing indecent material. Across the region, governments ignored him.

After *Noor*'s final episode, Turkish soap operas grew even more popular in the region and received glowing coverage from Arab and Western journalists. Beyond breaking cultural taboos, they displayed something else. In its soap operas, Turkey was modern, Muslim, and prosperous at the same time.

Premiering five years after *Noor, Magnificent Century* displays Turkey's growing economic power, cultural sophistication, and wealth. It is the most expensive TV program in Turkish history. Producers spend roughly $500,000 per episode, twice the amount that is spent on other serials. The program's launch party was held in Cannes, France. Its set is a lavish fifteen-room re-creation of Istanbul's Topkapi Palace, with real marble floors, handcrafted woodwork, and mock Ottoman and European throne rooms. Actors wear exquisite silk and velvet gowns crafted by a leading Turkish costume designer. Two siblings, known as the Coen brothers of Turkey, Durul and Yagmur Taylan, direct it.

"It's never been done before," Durul Taylan told me during a tour of the studio. "Not in this way."

In interviews, the directors and actors of *Magnificent Century* insisted the show was apolitical. "There is no political message or any other cultural message," said Ergenc, the actor who plays Suleiman. "This is a TV series. It is a soap opera."

Whether it is intentional or not, the makers of Turkey's soap operas are creating new roles, new heroes, and new cultural norms in a rapidly changing region.

As the Arab Spring unfolded, Turkey's political influence was on the rise as well. Erdogan was an early and vocal supporter of the Arab Spring uprisings. And after the toppling of dictators in Tunisia, Egypt, and Libya, he took a September 2011 victory tour of the region.

First, Erdogan and 260 Turkish businessmen made a historic visit to post-Mubarak Egypt. In a single day, the businessmen announced $853 million in new contracts with Egyptian companies. One of them, Davut Dogan, promised to build a new $10 million furniture manufacturing center.

"The factory will employ two hundred people," Dogan boasted in an interview several weeks later in Istanbul.

From the rapturous welcome Erdogan received to the economic power the Turkish businessmen displayed, the trip demonstrated Turkey's rise as a regional power. After visiting Cairo, Erdogan continued to Tunis and Tripoli. In all three newly liberated post–Arab Spring capitals, Erdogan did something that no American can do. The Turkish leader told captivated audiences that Islam and democracy could coexist. The devout Muslim head of a conservative, Islamist political party said Muslims could be pious and democratic.

"Islam and democracy are not contradictory," Erdogan declared in Tunis. "A Muslim can run a state very successfully."

One of the most popular leaders in the Middle East at the time, Erdogan had vastly more credibility in the region than Obama or any Western figure. Rightly or wrongly, he had turned himself into a folk hero by lambasting Israel. And his success at creating jobs was widely admired in countries desperate for economic growth.

Erdogan seemingly thwarted the two political dynamics that had haunted the region: ineffectual democracy and repressive military rule. To the amazement of many, he broke the grip of Turkey's military, which overthrew three civilian governments between 1960 and 1980. And his party became such a dominant force in Turkey's fractious political system that it ended a long series of weak coalition governments.

In 2011 elections, Erdogan's party won a third term with 49 percent of the vote, a historically high vote total in Turkey's splintered multiparty political system. Soon after, a parliamentary committee began drafting a new constitution to replace the one that had been drafted after a 1980 military coup.

In a 2011 interview, Mustafa Akyol, a Turkish newspaper columnist and frequent Erdogan defender, told me the prime minister's Justice and Development Party, known by its Turkish initials, AKP, was a model for Islamist parties in post–Arab Spring countries. Akyol's 2011 book, *Islam Without Extremes: A Muslim Case for Liberty*, argued that there can be liberalism within Islam and challenges the authoritarian interpretations of Iran, Saudi Arabia, and militant groups.

"We can speak of an AKP model for other Islamic parties—and that's a good model," Akyol said. "If more and more Islamists are inspired by the AKP model than by the totalitarian example of Iran, that will be good for the region."

Davut Dogan, the Turkish furniture magnate who traveled to Egypt with Erdogan, embodies the AKP's economic transformation of Turkey. The fifty-one-year-old's family furniture company is one of the so-called Anatolian tigers—burgeoning firms that have risen from Turkey's conservative heartland.

More religious, driven, and ruthless than the genteel Istanbul elite, Anatolian businessmen have helped fuel Turkey's economic surge. Dogan's company, Dogtas, has opened 115 stylish, IKEA-like stores across the country catering to upwardly mobile, smartphone-wielding middle-class Turks.

Dogtas has experienced extraordinary growth in the last five years, with sales revenues and employees doubling to $120 million and 1,300, respectively. The firm, launched thirty-nine years ago as a family business, now exports to sixty-five countries and plans to continue its aggressive expansion in the Middle East, where it already has twelve shops in Iran, seven in Libya, and two in Iraq.

"We want to be as big in Egypt," Dogan told me in 2011, "as we are in these other countries."

Bulent Celebi represents another type of growth in Turkey: high tech. Celebi, like Monis Rahman, the founder of Pakistan's first dating Web site, was profiled by American journalist Elmira Bayrasli in her magazine story on entrepreneurs in emerging market countries. Like Rahman, Celebi represents the intersection of technology, entrepreneurship, and globalization.

Istanbul is one of the world's most beautiful cities. It is also one of its most electronically impenetrable, Bayrasli wrote. The city's oldest houses are made of dense concrete that blocks the signals emitted by wireless routers designed for American drywall.

Sensing an opportunity, Celebi founded AirTies in 2004, an Istanbul technology start-up that develops and markets wireless electronic devices for specialized environments. After growing up in Istanbul, Celebi had moved to the United States and founded the chip company Ubicom in San Francisco, but memories of Istanbul and a business idea brought him home.

Celebi set out to create WiFi for the rest of the world. A WiFi box, just like a radio, streams a standard WiFi signal worldwide. But a standard American WiFi doesn't work everywhere, a fact that wireless giants Linksys, D-Link, and Netgear had not yet realized. Focused on the American market, none of U.S. firms were updating their devices for global markets. In San Francisco, Celebi encouraged U.S. firms to adapt their devices for emerging markets, which he believed would boom. When the companies ignored his advice, he set out to do it himself.

Using contacts he had developed in San Francisco, Celebi raised

$300,000 in seed capital from Silicon Valley investors and persuaded a handful of American-trained Turkish engineers to join him. First, Celebi concentrated on Istanbul, where the concrete floors and walls weakened a continuous wireless signal.

To solve the problem, he developed a mesh technology that sent out repeated pulses like a beating heart. Electronic devices were able to pick up the pulses without interruption, giving the user a better signal. That became Celebi's trademark, according to Bayrasli.

At the same time, he focused on service and customization, an area where Linksys and others also lagged. Targeting Turkey, the Balkans, and the Middle East, a combined market of 465 million, he created routers with manuals and twenty-four-hour customer support in Turkish, Arabic, Bulgarian, Greek, Kazakh, and Romanian. Then he added Russian, which, together with Ukrainian, added another 187 million potential customers.

In Turkey, Celebi's business quickly expanded beyond Istanbul to Anatolia, where telephones had become widespread only in the mid-1980s and cable did not reach televisions until the 1990s. For decades, Turkey had been considered a creative, technological, and economic laggard, according to Bayrasli. Through centuries of Ottoman rule, Turks had relegated trade, commerce, and business to Armenians, Greeks, and Jews.

In cold war Turkey, other problems emerged. Nepotism, red tape, weak rule of law, and a lack of investors and talent stifled Turkish markets, as they do in much of the developing world, Bayrasli wrote. Exhaustive bookkeeping to comply with Turkish tax laws and countless slips of paper that required business owners' personal authorization did as well. Last, under Turkish law, AirTies was Celebi's personal responsibility. There was no limited liability or protection. If the company failed, he and his family lost everything.

Starting in the 1990s, in an effort to finally secure a spot in the

European Union, Turkey's rulers slashed the country's bureaucracy and made it easier for Turks to register businesses, acquire licenses, build trade, and move capital freely in and out of the country. Turkish cotton traders struck deals with Levi's and Tommy Hilfiger. Anatolian furniture manufacturers like Dogtas signed deals with European conglomerates. Investment poured in, and a middle class was born. In a virtuous circle, Turkey's emerging middle class allowed Celebi to push entrepreneurship further.

Before becoming a senior adviser to Richard Holbrooke, Vali Nasr described the process in a 2009 book, *Forces of Fortune: The Rise of the New Muslim Middle Class and What It Will Mean for Our World*.

"Economic power shifted to small- and medium-sized businesses," Nasr wrote, "and the Anatolian heartland overshadowed Istanbul as an engine of growth."

Today AirTies dominates the wireless router market in the region, boasting 50 percent of the wireless market share in Turkey alone, according to Bayrasli. It generates millions in revenues and is planning on an initial public offering in the next few years.

Today Turkey is the world's eighteenth-largest economy—bigger than all but a handful of the twenty-seven actual EU nations that have kept Turkey waiting for accession for decades. To many Turks, EU membership is no longer important. They see their future in the global market.

In the spring of 2013, Erdogan's response to the Taksim Square protests deeply divided Turkish society and destroyed his credibility internationally. Accusing foreign powers of secretly conspiring against Turkey, he declared the demonstrators "criminals" and had riot police clear the square. Four people died, eleven struck by tear gas canisters were blinded, and an estimated eight thousand were injured in weeks of clashes that spanned the country.

The move drove up support for Erdogan among members of his socially conservative political party. But it infuriated secular Turks, who chafed under his increasingly authoritarian rule.

What was unusual about the demonstrations was that they involved young, well-educated Turks who were the beneficiaries of Erdogan's economic boom. Alper, a twenty-six-year-old Turkish corporate lawyer, is typical. The young protester, who asked that his last name not be published because he feared arrest, is one of millions of young professionals who rode the country's economic growth to a lifestyle his grandparents could scarcely imagine. Yet he loathed Erdogan.

"The prime minister is continuing to blatantly lie about the demonstrations," he told me in a June 2013 telephone interview. "People are actually scared that if they stop this momentum, then the government will feel free to exercise more force."

The protests were not pitched battles between religious conservatives and secular liberals. Instead, they were deeply Turkish. After decades of the Turkish state reigning supreme, young Turks demanded pluralism and basic individual rights. They called for the Turkish state to be accountable to the people, instead of the people being accountable to the state.

"Basic freedoms such as the right to peaceful assembly are undermined by police and government," Alper said in a later e-mail. "There have been no significant repercussions for police officers and their superiors."

The government targeted the media as well. Using vague and antiquated security and defamation laws, Turkey jailed forty journalists in 2013, more than any other country in the world, including China, Iran, and Eritrea. Fearing government retaliation, the owners of media companies fired outspoken journalists. Many reporters engaged in self-censorship. Erdogan set the tone, publicly denigrating journalists by name.

Mustafa Akyol, the columnist who praised Erdogan in 2011, condemned his response to Taksim but said reports of totalitarianism were exaggerated. "Turkey is not on the path to becoming another Iran or Saudi Arabia—or something like Vladimir Putin's Russia," he wrote in November 2013. "But it certainly is not a fully liberal democracy yet."

Others thought the crackdown could help opposition parties fare better at the polls. For years, Soli Ozel, a professor of international relations and political science at Istanbul Bilgi University, scoffed at Westerners who viewed Turkey as a model for the Middle East. The protests, however, make him feel the label may apply.

"After this unprecedented mobilization," he said in a June 2013 telephone interview, "we now have a very vibrant and very much alive civil society."

The question was no longer whether Erdogan's Turkey was a model for the region. It was whether a post-Erdogan Turkey could be. With a new leader, Turkey represents the ability of Western technology, consumerism, entrepreneurship, and investment to transform a country. And, unlike Iraq and Afghanistan, it is a potentially powerful example of a new interpretation of Islam fashioned by Muslims, not outsiders.

CHAPTER 6

The Silicon Valley of the Arab World?

In June 2009, President Obama called for "a new beginning" between the United States and the Muslim world in a historic speech at Cairo University. No one present—including Obama—had any sense of the sweeping changes about to be unleashed across the region.

In his speech, Obama called for mutual respect, the spread of democracy, and peace between Israelis and Palestinians. As millions of Arabs watched, he also promised revitalized economic aid.

"On economic development, we will create a new corps of business volunteers to partner with counterparts in Muslim-majority countries," Obama said. "And I will host a Summit on Entrepreneurship this year to identify how we can deepen ties between business leaders, foundations, and social entrepreneurs in the United States and Muslim communities around the world."

In April 2010, the administration held the promised summit in Washington and launched a series of programs to send American businessmen, investors, and scientists to the Middle East. Eight months later, a twenty-six-year-old Tunisian street vendor named Mohamed Bouazizi doused himself in gasoline on December 10, set himself on fire, and sparked the Arab Spring.

The protests, though, were not as spontaneous as they seemed. For months, unemployment and food prices had been rising in Tunisia as the global economy slowed. And the November 2010 release by WikiLeaks of secret American diplomatic cables detailing staggering corruption by Tunisian President Zine el-Abidine Ben Ali stoked popular anger as well. The cables also gave protesters the sense that American support for Ben Ali was waning.

Twenty-eight days after the largely peaceful protests began, Ben Ali fled the country. Obama, who felt that he had been too passive during the June 2009 uprising in Iran, made no effort to help Ben Ali. The president's move was both courageous and practical. Tunisia, a small country that was not strategically important to the United States, was a low-risk place to support a revolution. Few American officials thought the uprisings would spread.

Secretary of State Hillary Clinton and European diplomats praised the revolution but offered limited financial support to the country's new government. European Union countries pledged $300 million in direct assistance. The Obama administration, which saw Tunisia as Europe's responsibility, offered roughly the same amount.

Ten months after Ben Ali's ouster, the American embassy announced that a delegation of American high-tech entrepreneurs and angel investors would be visiting Tunisia. American officials, it seemed, were delivering on Obama's promise in Cairo to bring U.S. entrepreneurs to the region. The group would hold a workshop on launching start-ups, listen to attendees' business proposals, and then choose one Tunisian for training and mentoring in the United States.

The response was overwhelming. Dozens of Tunisian entrepreneurs, programmers, and engineers applied to attend the session. Each applicant submitted a written proposal for a new start-up. The organizers then invited the authors of the fifty best proposals to attend.

From beginning to end, the workshop overflowed with energy. Young Tunisians clamored to speak with the American entrepreneurs and investors. When a young woman's proposal for a biotech start-up was finally chosen as the winner, other attendees were disappointed. Privately, members of the American delegation were disappointed as well.

In truth, the post-Cairo initiative that brought them to Tunisia operated on a shoestring. The program—Partners for a New Beginning—was so poorly funded that members of the delegation had to pay their own airfare and hotel bills. The U.S. government did not propose, fund, or carry out the training of the winning entrepreneur. Members of the delegation did. And the prize? Three months in the TechTown incubator in Detroit, Michigan, courtesy of TechTown, Wayne State University, and the American Arab Chamber of Commerce in Detroit.

One member of the delegation, Sami Ben Romdhane, a Tunisian American eBay executive, was shocked by the lack of funding. A founder of two Silicon Valley start-ups and former Apple and Oracle employee, Ben Romdhane was impressed by the talent pool in Tunisia.

"There is a lot of potential," Ben Romdhane said in a telephone interview after his visit. "I don't see any difference between students who are graduating there and students who are graduating here and in Europe."

The administration's tepid effort showed how the United States was missing an opportunity in Tunisia to create a post–Arab Spring success story. More broadly, it was evidence that the administration was taking the wrong lessons from Afghanistan, Iraq, and Pakistan and squandering the opportunity that the Arab Spring created.

In interviews, Tunisians embraced Obama's message in Cairo. Asked what the United States could do to help Tunisia, they called for increased American business investment, tourism, and educational exchange programs, not traditional foreign aid.

Without prompting, they disparaged hard-line Salafists who had emerged since the toppling of Ben Ali in January 2011. Declaring themselves a model for the rest of the Middle East, Tunisians said they yearned for prosperity, modernity, and a place in the global economy.

Public opinion polls showed a deep distrust of the United States. A 2012 survey found that 90 percent of Tunisians wanted democracy in their country but believed that the United States had not supported their revolution. A year after Obama's Cairo speech, only 40 percent of Tunisians had a positive view of the U.S. president. In Washington, Obama himself was disappointed by how few of his promises in Cairo had been turned into functioning programs. The government's weak civilian institutions had again failed at implementation.

"Obama later conceded that the speech was longer on promises than on deliverables," journalist David E. Sanger wrote in his 2012 book, *Confront and Conceal*. "A year later, when he asked for an assessment of how well the administration had implemented the ideas he announced in Cairo, he was, in the words of one aide, "deeply disappointed in how little got done."

In Tunisia, meanwhile, the country's postrevolution economy collapsed. In 2011, the growth rate dropped from 3 percent to -1.8 percent, inflation nearly doubled to 5 percent, foreign investment declined by 30 percent, and the country's tourism industry disappered. In 2012, the economy improved somewhat, growing at 3.6 percent, but Tunisia's growth remained half the 5 percent growth it enjoyed between 1997 and 2007.

The Islamist political party that won the country's first post–Ben Ali elections—Ennahda, or the "Renaissance Party"—struggled to effectively run the government after decades in exile. The party's charismatic leader was Rached Ghannouchi, a seventy-year-old Sorbonne-educated Islamist intellectual who had spent fourteen years in Tunisian prisons and twenty-two years in exile in London.

In an interview, Ghannouchi described his Ennahda party as a moderate Islamist movement modeled after Turkish Prime Minister Erdogan's AKP party. He said he fervently supported democracy, a stand that put him at odds with radical Salafists who consider democracy an affront to God's authority. Echoing Turkish moderates, he said democracy and Islam were not only compatible, they follow the same traditions.

"The real spokesman of Islam is public opinion, which is the high authority, the highest authority," he said. "Legislation, represented by the assembly, the national assembly."

Ghannouchi said the prophet Muhammad's use of *shuras*—or councils—to make nonreligious decisions showed that democracy had existed in Islam since its birth. Government affairs should be decided by democratic vote, he said, not fatwas from religious autocrats. And he embraced free-market capitalism, full rights for women and minorities, and international human rights treaties.

Secular Tunisians, though, say that Ghannouchi's party has not followed those ideals since gaining power. The party proposed that the country's new draft constitution have a blasphemy law in it that makes insulting any of the three Abrahamic faiths a crime. To secular Tunisians, this is a clear limit on free speech.

In February 2012, the party stood by when a Tunisian judge jailed a newspaper editor for eight days after he published a photograph of a soccer player and his nude girlfriend on the cover of a local tabloid. And in April 2012, two young men were sentenced to seven years in jail for posting cartoons of a nude prophet Muhammad on Facebook. One fled to France. The other was jailed.

Secular Tunisians said they no longer trust Ennahda. Ahmed Ounaies, a Tunisian politician who briefly served as foreign minister in the country's postrevolutionary unity government, was typical. In an interview, he said he no longer believed Ghannouchi. He said that purportedly moderate Muslim leaders were, in fact, aligned with hard-line Islamists.

"We believe that Mr. Ghannouchi is a Salafist," Ounaies said. "He is a real supporter of those groups."

Amid the political and economic turmoil, hard-line Tunisian Salafists have became increasingly emboldened. In 2011, they attacked a television station in Tunis after it aired the animated film *Persepolis,* which featured what they considered a blasphemous portrayal of God. They attacked liquor stores and art galleries. They held protests that paralyzed the country's leading university for a month. And in the capital they climbed a historic bell tower and waved jihadist flags from its spire—an image that unnerved Tunisian moderates and foreign investors.

Clashes and demonstrations continued in 2012. In May, one of the country's new Salafist groups, Ansar al-Shariah, held a rally in the religious city of Kairouan. At the event, Salafists dressed in the style of Afghan Taliban staged martial arts demonstrations and horsemen brandished swords.

In June, they attacked an art exhibit in Tunis, setting off clashes across the country and a three-day curfew. And after the amateur video insulting the prophet Muhammad emerged in September 2012, several thousand Salafists attacked the American embassy in Tunis and burned down the adjacent American school. The following day, the State Department announced that the families of all American diplomats and other nonessential personnel would be evacuated from the country.

The news devastated secular Tunisians. They were furious at Tunisia's new government for failing to deploy enough police to protect the embassy. And they were surprised that the United States reacted so drastically to a protest by a small faction of Tunisians.

Sami Ben Romdhane, the Tunisian American eBay executive, said Tunisians who prided themselves on being one of the most liberal societies in the Middle East felt abandoned.

"Now it's official," Ben Romdhane told me. "We are being treated as a terrorist country and a place where Americans are not safe. That hurt a lot of people in the country."

Tunisian moderates argued that the United States was missing an opportunity in Tunisia. America's strongest weapons against militancy were engagement, investment, and technology, they said. Young Tunisians yearned to work in the new, high-tech offices that Hewlett-Packard, Fidelity, Microsoft, and Cisco opened in Tunisia in recent years. They dreamed of turning their country into a regional hub for cloud, big-data, and open-government computing.

Leila Charfi, the head of the Microsoft Innovation Center in Tunis, helped organize the visit by the American high-tech delegation. She said Facebook and Twitter had facilitated the street protests that toppled Ben Ali, and that Tunisians now embraced technology. "People are hungry to use new technology and develop a new country with IT," she said.

But after the attack on the American embassy, investors from Silicon Valley and Europe saw Tunisia as unstable and anti-American, according to Ben Romdhane.

"They're asking, 'What happened? How come this country changed in eighteen months and became like Libya?'" Ben Romdhane said. "I keep saying, 'This is not representative. This is a fraction of a percent of people.'"

The change in perception is alarming. Prior to the embassy attack, American diplomats believed that Tunisia had the brightest long-term prospects of any Arab Spring country. It has an ethnically homogeneous population of only 10 million, a long history of moderation, and centuries of trade with Europe that have created a strong business class and millions of bilingual Arabic and French speakers.

Most important, the country's lack of oil forced it to develop a multifaceted economy after it achieved independence from France in 1956. Its universities graduate six thousand engineers a year, and Tunisian entrepreneurs managed to develop niche markets in Europe. Inspired by Jean Touitou, the Tunisian-born designer and founder of the French clothing line A.P.C., Tunisian factories cornered the market on rush orders from Europe for high-quality clothes. Tunisian auto-parts factories produced high-quality components for Mercedes-Benz and other elite car manufacturers. And the country's farms provided Europe with everything from fresh vegetables to olive oil.

Like that of Turkey, Tunisia's economy eventually became closely tied to that of Europe. France, the former colonial power, was Tunisia's largest foreign investor. As a result, when the European sovereign debt crisis exploded in 2010, Tunisia was one of the victims. As European orders and investment dropped, unemployment and food prices rose in Tunisia. Europe offered little aid to Tunisia as well. The tepid postrevolutionary economy exacerbated a festering economic divide between Tunisia's wealthy coast and impoverished interior. When I visited Tunisia fourteen months after the revolution, in March 2012, I found pockets of simmering anger and a deep sense of unmet expectations. Tunisians who had expected a postrevolutionary gold rush held protests and wildcat strikes on a daily basis.

In the southern town of Gafsa, unemployed people blocked roads to the town's phosphate mine, the fifth largest in the world, and demanded jobs. Production had dropped by 40 percent. After wildcat strikes by local workers, a Japanese company shut down its local factory. A German company threatened to do the same.

Even in Sidi Bouzid, the farming town where Tunisia's uprising began, the luster of the revolution had faded. The manager of a call center that a French investor had opened to help support the revolution complained of constant confrontations with workers. Whenever she tried to fire someone, their parents came to the office and berated her. Strikes occurred constantly at other businesses, she said, sowing chaos.

On a dusty street, eighty-five-year-old Ahmad Kadachi said he was also disillusioned. The dean of the town's street vendors, Kadachi had been astonished when Bouazizi, the local vendor, had set himself on fire and sparked the Arab Spring.

As Kadachi sold tea from his ramshackle wooden cart, he called Bouazizi a hothead, but thanked him for the freedom he had brought. Now, Kadachi said, he was frustrated with postrevolutionary Tunisia. He said Tunisians enjoyed being able to choose their leaders and express their opinions, but a primary goal of their revolutions eluded them: prosperity.

"Everybody is talking and talking," Kadachi told me. "No one is doing anything."

In Tunis, the country's cosmopolitan capital, the verdict on the revolution was more positive. Khalil Zahouani, a thirty-four-year-old

Tunisian entrepreneur, said the ouster of Ben Ali had perfectly positioned Tunisia to follow India's example and become an outsourcing hub for the region. With millions of well-educated French speakers, Tunisia could become the French-speaking world's back office, Zahouani said. In Tunisia, software companies, call centers, and engineering firms could perform tasks at a fraction of the cost of Europe.

Zahouani's own experience was an example. After graduating from a Swiss university and working in Geneva for several years, he returned to Tunisia to start his own business. Like Monis Rahman, the American-educated Pakistani entrepreneur who returned home to start Pakistan's first online dating site, Zahouani believed that his chances of creating a fast-growing technology company were higher in Tunisia than in Europe. When I met him in Tunis, Zahouani ran a seventy-person start-up that provided computing services to European and Arab phone conglomerates.

His firm, Dot IT, is based in Les Berges du Lac, one of Tunis's priciest neighborhoods. It felt global. Young, cigarette-smoking Tunisian couples clad in stylish French clothes filled a nearby bistro. A sushi restaurant was a few blocks away.

As Zahouani spoke excitedly of his business plan, several dozen young men and women clad in Western clothes worked intently at their computers. Some women wore headscarves. Some did not.

"We can have centers for excellence for IBM, Apple, and Google for the region," Zahouani predicted. "It could be an outsourcing hub."

A few miles away, Hewlett-Packard, the Palo Alto, California–based computing giant, and SunGard, a Wayne, Pennsylvania–based software company, share a sparkling new office building. With subsidies from the Ben Ali government, the two companies built an ultramodern office complex several years ago. On the building's ground floor was a gym with yoga classes, a gleaming new cafeteria, and an employee lounge with a large-screen television. Workers were dressed casually in jeans and button-down shirts. Young Tunisians from across the country competed fiercely to work at the two firms. Both were seen as doorways to the global economy.

In SunGard's lobby, clocks displayed the current time in the company's Tunis, New York, and Pune, India, offices. Worldwide, SunGard had seventeen thousand employees in seventy countries. Last year, it earned roughly $4.5 billion providing software and processing services for financial companies, governments, and educational institutions.

In Tunis, its five hundred employees performed back-office work for French- and English-speaking customers in Europe, Asia, and North America. It was also a beachhead for the company in the 200-million-strong Middle Eastern market.

Adel Torjmen, SunGard's managing director in Tunisia, said private investment from American companies was much more valuable than American government development aid.

"What the U.S. can bring is very clear," he said. "The savior of Tunisia cannot be the government of the United States. It is the private sector."

Torjmen, a Tunisian engineer educated in France, said the problem was not that Tunisia had a negative image in the United States. It was that it had no image at all in the United States. American companies do not think of the Middle East, he said, when they consider outsourcing. If IBM moved only 15 percent of its 150,000 employees in India to Tunisia, he said, it would make a vast difference in the country's economy.

"Tunisia can be yet another Dubai but addressing Europe and Africa," he said. "Our cost structure is better than Morocco and we are close to India. Try to give us a kind of privilege, a kind of chance."

Radhi Meddeb, a French- and Italian-educated Tunisian engineer who heads the Action and Solidarity Development Association, a leading Tunisian nonprofit development group, said American business expertise was needed as well. Meddeb said Tunisia needed help restructuring its banking sector, creating a microfinance system, forming public-private partnerships to build infrastructure, and creating a private equity fund.

He called for a $25 billion American investment over the next seven to ten years in modernizing Tunisia's infrastructure. Someday, he hoped, Tunisia and the United States could sign a free-trade agreement.

Regarding Europe, Meddeb said Tunisia should voluntarily enact the reforms mandated in the EU accession process but not expect admission, given Europe's financial crisis. The United States and Europe had promised $20 billion in aid to Tunisia and Egypt at the 2011 G8 summit in Deauville, he said, but little of that money had arrived.

Meddeb and other Tunisians complained as the economy sputtered that the Ennahda-led government was spending enormous amounts of time debating the status of religion in the country's new constitution. Unlike Erdogan, who managed the Turkish economy deftly, Ennahda seems overwhelmed. Secular Tunisians said Ennahda needed to crack down on the Salafists immediately.

Ghannouchi, Ennahda's leader, played down the country's divisions and called for patience.

"I am not pessimistic," he said in the interview. "There is a chance to reach a compromise."

In February 2013, members of an extremist cell linked to al-Qaeda assassinated leftist politician Chokri Belaid. In July 2013, the same group shot dead opposition leader Mohamed Brahmi in front of his family. The killings sparked a campaign of sit-ins, walk-outs, and rallies by the secular opposition. Ennahda responded with rallies of its own. As political polarization rose, Ennahda agreed to new elections in the spring of 2014.

The United States needs to engage more with Tunisia. So far, the Obama administration has provided $350 million in aid to Tunisia, which includes security force training and $100 million in Tunisian government budget support. The American effort should be larger and more innovative.

Tunisia remains the region's best chance for a post–Arab Spring success story. State Department officials are overreacting to their expensive failures in Afghanistan, Iraq, and Pakistan and shifting to a minimalist approach.

In conversations, American diplomats in Tunis focused on limiting their aid efforts and engaging in only traditional diplomacy. Many of them had served in Iraq or Afghanistan and saw the aid programs there as wasteful aberrations that departed from the State Department's true diplomatic mission.

They are mistaken.. The State Department must be more innovative and learn how to devise, properly fund, and implement programs like the one that brought Ben Romdhane and the other Arab American entrepreneurs to Tunis. Facilitating investment, entrepreneurship, and educational exchanges on a vast scale should be a core element of the State Department's mission. The Tunisian businessmen I spoke with were correct. American investment, consumerism, and technology are our most powerful tools against militancy. The United States should engage in traditional diplomacy in Tunisia, but also focus intently on economic growth.

In interviews, Tunisian Islamists said they did not want American meddling in their political affairs, but they were eager to be part of the world economy. Becoming Hamas-like international pariahs seemed to hold little appeal for them. They too know that a by-product of a globalized economy is that isolation now carries a staggering economic cost.

Asked what U.S. policies would most help Muslim moderates, Ennahda founder Ghannouchi echoed secular Tunisians. He called for the U.S. government to "encourage investment," "encourage tourism," and sharply expand training and educational exchange programs. Asked what U.S. policies were most destructive, he said that unilateral U.S. military interventions undermine Muslim moderates.

Since taking power after the revolution, Tunisia's Islamists were repeatedly undermined by the actions of hard-line radicals. "Ennahda's nearly two-year journey in government has been one of steady concessions and backing down," the *New York Times* reported in September 2013. "And it has been a sharp lesson for the Islamists: their party has been most weakened by extremist Islamists linked to Al Qaeda."

Whether it was due to a willingness to compromise or a lack of political strength, Tunisia's Islamists proved less confrontational than politicians in other countries. The culture of compromise taking hold across Tunisia's political spectrum is the country's best hope for stability. It is also a vital example for the region.

CHAPTER 7

Murder in Benghazi

In September 2011, Mark Ward, a fifty-seven-year-old senior USAID official, arrived in Tripoli after spending much of the last decade in Afghanistan and Pakistan. Ward, a San Francisco native, father of two sons, and former lawyer had seen the mistakes of the American effort in Afghanistan and Pakistan firsthand. In Libya, he was determined to get the American aid effort right.

From 2002 to 2003, Ward had served as USAID mission director in Pakistan. In 2005, he returned to Pakinstan to coordinate US-AID's response to a devastating earthquake in the country's north. From 2006 to 2008, Ward lived in Washington and served as the agency's head of procurement, overseeing its army of contractors in Afghanistan and Iraq. From 2008 to 2010, he was seconded to the UN and moved to Kabul while serving as the organization's senior adviser for development.

In 2009, Ward narrowly survived a Taliban attack on the UN guesthouse where he lived in Kabul. Five UN staff and three Afghans were killed. Ward and twenty-five other survivors owed their lives to a young American who worked as Ward's UN security guard. Louis Maxwell, a twenty-seven-year-old father of two and former navy sailor from Florida, grabbed his weapon as soon as the attack began. Running to the roof, Maxwell held off three suicide bombers who were trying to enter the compound. After Ward and two dozen others fled, Maxwell was shot dead.

"He was a wonderful guy," Ward recalled. "He really was a hero. I told my boys there are not many of us who get to meet a real hero and I did."

Ward arrived in Tripoli in September 2011 and immediately warmed to Libya and Libyans. He spent the next thirteen months advising UN, American, and European officials on how to better coordinate foreign aid projects. In Afghanistan, a free-for-all had ensued. With little to no input from Afghan officials, foreign countries built hundreds of projects that impressed their bosses back home but didn't necessarily aid Afghans. With no coordinated strategy, waste was endemic.

Two things in Libya immediately struck Ward as completely different from Afghanistan. The country was overflowing with oil wealth. As a result, Libyan officials did not hesitate to tell foreign officials what was on their minds.

"The transitional government officials that I worked with were very capable of saying no," Ward recalled, "to what they perceived as a bad idea."

Libya has an estimated 46 billion barrels of oil, one of the largest reserves in the world. Its population is small but well educated, with a 89 percent literacy rate among its 6.7 million people. During and after the uprising against Qaddafi, the United States and other countries gave the country's interim government control of $100 billion in Libyan government and Qaddafi family assets seized abroad.

The differences between Libya and Afghanistan leapt out at Ward. In Kabul, he had watched in frustration as Afghan officials said yes to expensive foreign aid projects that their government would be unable to maintain in the future. In Tripoli, Libyan officials promised to reimburse the U.S. government for any training they received.

"They said we need U.S. expertise, not your money," Ward recalled.

And when a foreigner pushed too far, the Libyans made their feelings clear.

"I used to tell people, 'From my own personal experience, we've got to just chill here,'" Ward told me. "The way we are going to build trust with the Libyans is listening to them."

Some foreign diplomats ignored his advice. Others completely agreed. One senior diplomat who shared Ward's go-slow approach was the new U.S. ambassador to Libya, J. Christopher Stevens.

Stevens, like Ward, was a Northern California native and former lawyer who became a diplomat. While Ward focused on South Asia, Stevens spent twenty years working across the Middle East. In 2011, Stevens had lived with rebels in Benghazi and made sure that U.S. aid reached the Libyan opposition. Ward and Stevens both spent hours talking to Libyans and trying to understand the country.

"He represented what you hoped would be the model of a new American diplomat," Ward said. "He was much happier rolling his sleeves up and going to work and talking to Libyans."

The Libyans were deeply suspicious of the United States and Europe. After decades of being an international pariah, Qaddafi was embraced by President George W. Bush and British Prime Minister Tony Blair in 2004 after halting Libya's nuclear weapons program and handing over its chemical weapons. In 2006, the United States established full diplomatic relations with the Libyan government, turning a blind eye to nearly forty years of brutal Qaddafi family rule.

Behind the scenes, Blair had helped negotiate oil exploration deals worth at least $500 million for the British conglomerate Royal Dutch Shell. U.S. oil companies descended on Libya as well, along with other Americans in search of profit. Monitor, a Boston-based consulting group run by Harvard Business School professors, received $3 million from the Qaddafi regime from 2006 to 2008 to help rehabilitate Qaddafi's image in the United States.

Monitor paid travel expenses, consulting fees, and honorariums to conservative American scholars such as Francis Fukuyama and Richard Perle, as well as liberals like Benjamin Barber, Joseph Nye, and Robert Putnam. At Monitor's expense the prominent Americans visited Qaddafi and wrote stories about him. The firm also helped ghostwrite the PhD thesis of one of Qaddafi's son's, Saif, at the London School of Economics.

Qaddafi's repression, meanwhile, continued. For decades, Qaddafi ruled by pitting Libyans against one another. An estimated 10 to 20 percent of the population served in various overlapping surveillance directorates that monitored Libyans in government agencies, factories, and schools. The police state extended beyond Libya. During the 1980s, a network of diplomats and recruits killed twenty-five opponents of Qaddafi in foreign countries.

Over the years, Qaddafi's behavior grew more bizarre. In 2009, he gave a ninety-minute speech to the United Nations General Assembly in New York. At different points in the rambling address, he called for the reinvestigation of the killings of John F. Kennedy and Martin Luther King Jr., the creation of a joint Israeli-Palestinian state called "Isratine," and hailed Barack Obama, whom he called a "son of Africa."

"Obama is a glimpse in the darkness after four or eight years," he said. "We are content and happy if Obama can stay forever as president of the United States."

After Qaddafi's death in 2011, President Obama issued clear orders that the United States should not lead the postwar stabilization effort in Libya. In Tripoli, European diplomats coordinated the international effort while U.S. diplomats took a secondary role. It was an example of Obama's belief in focusing American resources on direct threats to the United States and handing over responsibility to allies when possible.

"What I saw was a United States that was in listening mode, that was very much waiting for the Libyans to say, 'This is where we need help,'" Ward recalled. "And resisting what maybe is our more traditional approach, which is supply side assistance, 'This is what you need, and we have it, so can we provide it?'"

One final dynamic that was different from Afghanistan was that of security contractors. After seeing reports of their aggressive behavior, Libyan officials blocked the United States from using firms like Blackwater to protect its diplomats. The CIA and State Department hired a dozen private contractors to roam the country and buy looted anti-aircraft missiles that could fall into the hands of militants. But security contractors were barred.

Obama's desire to stay out of post-conflict Libya was a reflection of his determination to prevent the United States from getting embroiled in another Mideast conflict. He was initially skeptical of a military intervention and his aides were deeply divided.

In March 2011, Qaddafi loyalists were on the verge of taking Benghazi, a city of seven hundred thousand and the capital of the rebellion. A massacre was expected, with Qaddafi declaring the rebels "cockroaches" and "traitors."

Defense Secretary Robert Gates urged caution along with national security adviser Tom Donilon and counterterrorism chief John Brennan. They argued that Libya was not vital to American national security interests, the *New York Times* reported. Brennan worried that the Libyan rebels might have links to al-Qaeda.

United Nations ambassador Susan Rice, who had served as the State Department's top Africa official during the Rwanda genocide, supported U.S. military action. The deciding voice was Clinton's. In an unusual split with Gates, the secretary of state called for U.S. participation in air strikes after Arab and European states agreed to join them and the United Nations Security Council authorized the use of force.

Obama insisted on one caveat: no American ground troops in Libya. In a subsequent interview, Ben Rhodes, Obama's deputy national security adviser for strategic communications, told me that ending American military interventions in the region remained the administration's primary goal.

"One big part of this administration's foreign policy legacy is going to be ending the wars," Rhodes said, referring to Iraq and Afghanistan. "We're not interested in getting involved in more wars."

After the fall of Qaddafi, Libya was plagued by tribal divisions. While Tunisia is relatively homogenous ethnically, Libya is a conglomeration of North African tribes that were cobbled together by colonial mapmakers. It lacks the strong national identities and revered national leaders that modern Turkey and Tunisia enjoyed in Mustafa Kemal Ataturk and Habib Bourguiba.

When the 2011 uprising against Qaddafi began, hundreds of militias formed along tribal lines. After his death, militias refused to disarm or hand over an estimated five thousand prisoners they had declared regime loyalists. Human rights groups gained access to some of the prisoners. Their stories were grim. Captives said the militias engaged in torture, held prisoners without evidence, and blocked detainees from seeing judges for up to a year.

The country's National Transitional Council—which Libyan

exiles dominated—impressed Ward. The council's leaders moved cautiously, dealt with immediate crises, did not confront militias, and waited for an elected government to set policy. When firefights between rival militias broke out in parts of the country, the interim council dispatched envoys to negotiate truces.

The Transitional Council also embraced the emergence of Libyan women's, human rights, and press groups. They welcomed protests. During one of Ward's meetings with the deputy prime minister, gunfire erupted outside. The Libyan official smiled and said the shooting was a healthy sign.

"He sat back in his chair and he had this big smile on his face," Ward recalled. "He said, 'Isn't this great? This is what we fought for.'"

Four months after Ward left Libya, the country held its first free elections in four decades, in June 2012. More than three thousand candidates—including women—competed for two hundred seats in a new assembly. To the astonishment of many, a coalition of liberals led by National Transitional Council leader Mahmoud Jibril won thirty-nine of the eighty seats for political parties. Jibril's party even won in Darnah, the suicide bomber stronghold. The Muslim Brotherhood came in second, with seventeen.

One surprise winner was Hassan al-Amin, an exiled Libyan human rights activist. In parliament, al-Amin conducted investigations into abuses by militias.

When Ward completed his assignment and returned to Washington in February 2012, he believed the United States had struck the right balance in Libya. It was listening to the new government and waiting for it to make specific requests from the international community, something that rarely happened in Afghanistan, Iraq, and Pakistan. Ward credited Obama with setting the right tone. He said a UN colleague praised the United States for showing unusual restraint.

"The United States was handling this the right way," Ward recalled. "The United States can lead even when it's not leading."

At 9:15 P.M. on September 11, 2012, Ambassador Chris Stevens finished a meeting with the Turkish ambassador, walked him to the front gate of the American consulate in Benghazi, and bid him good night. Stevens briefly chatted with the compound's Libyan guards. Three were armed members of a local militia that had rebelled against the Qaddafi regime. Four were unarmed. Then Stevens returned to his residence.

Fifteen minutes later, the guards heard shouts of "God is great!" outside the compound. At first, they thought a funeral procession might have been passing by. Then one of them heard an American shouting, "Attack, attack," over the radio. Gunfire erupted and grenades began landing in the center of the compound.

In a carefully coordinated assault, several dozen members of Ansar al-Shariah, a well-known local militia consisting of hard-line Islamic militants, were attacking the compound. Armed with rocket-propelled grenades and truck-mounted artillery, they fired grenade after grenade into the compound.

"They thought that there would be more Americans inside, commandos or something like that," Mohamed Bishari, a twenty-year-old neighbor who watched the attack, told the *New York Times*. "So they immediately started attacking with their RPG rockets."

In truth, seven Americans were inside the compound and only four of them were armed. One of Mr. Stevens's bodyguards ran out of an office building holding a light weapon and sprinted to Stevens's residence under fire, according to Libyan guards. Two other armed Americans climbed on a rooftop and fought back against the attackers. So did the armed Libyan fighters.

Inside his residence, Stevens, a technician named Sean Smith, and Stevens's bodyguard locked themselves in a secure safe room. At some point, the attackers breached the compound, poured diesel around Stevens's residence, and set it ablaze.

What happened next is unclear. As thick smoke filled the safe room, the three Americans apparently tried to make a run for it. The bodyguard climbed out a window, but Stevens and Smith succumbed to the smoke and died of asphyxiation. In the chaos, guards found Smith's body but were unable to locate Stevens. Four hours later, two guards died in a carefully planned mortar attack in a CIA compound a mile away.

Stevens was the first American ambassador to be killed in an act of terrorism in twenty-three years. His death immediately became a heated issue in the 2012 presidential campaign. Republicans accused the Obama administration of failing to provide adequate security for American diplomats. They also accused the White House of trying to downplay the attack by initially calling it a spontaneous demonstration sparked by the amateur American-made anti-Muslim video. The Obama administration denied both charges.

Within twenty-four hours, the State Department pulled all of its diplomats out of Libya. The suffocating security that hindered the civilian effort in Afghanistan, Pakistan, and Iraq grew even more intense. What happened in Benghazi and how to respond to it consumed Washington.

Over the next several weeks, press reports and congressional investigations revealed that midlevel State Department officials had denied repeated requests for additional security in Benghazi as attacks rose in the summer of 2012. Barred from using contractors, the department's Diplomatic Security Service had such a small staff that it sent its personnel to Libya on three-month rotations.

At one point in the summer, the Benghazi compound had only one American guard. State Department officials said Benghazi was a symbol of a brittle, overstretched, and underfunded State Department.

When Ward learned of Stevens's death, he was dismayed but thought that Stevens's wishes would be clear.

"He would say to the American people, please don't turn your back on Libya," Ward told me. "They've been through forty terrible years, they've just held elections, and they've rejected extremism. This is absolutely not the time to let a couple of lunatics throw us off our resolve."

According to Ward, Stevens's message to Libyans would be to arrest the suspected perpetrators, provide them with defense lawyers, and give them a fair trial. "Do the right thing," Ward said. "If there is one thing [his] life should stand for, let it stand for the rule of law."

A week after Stevens's murder, an estimated thirty thousand Benghazi residents took to the streets of the city, protested Stevens's death, and called for the disbanding of militias. That night, protesters stormed the compound of Ansar al-Shariah and forced them to flee.

"We want police in the streets; we don't want the militia," Nisa Nejam, a twenty-one-year-old blogger and civil society activist who participated in the protest, said in a telephone interview. "We want all of them under the control of the government."

But Libya's central government remained divided and weak. No major militias were disarmed. In some areas, new militias emerged American officials had provided $170 million in aid to Libya after the fall of Qaddafi, but the oil-rich nation's problem was not a lack of funds. It was a lack of government security forces. As in Iraq and Afghanistan, establishing law and order had emerged as the key priority in post-conflict Libya.

As lawlessness spread, American Special Forces soldiers arrested a senior al-Qaeda operative on the streets of Tripoli in October 2013. Islamic hardliners accused Libya's moderate, democratically elected prime minister, Ali Zeidan, of cooperating with the United States. A week later, Zeidan himself was kidnapped for several hours by a militia in Tripoli. He was released unhurt but militias continued to ignore his orders to leave Tripoli.

By the fall of 2013, many Libyans had given up on the new government. "Libyans are basically fed up," al-Amin, the human rights activist who was elected to parliament, told me in a telephone interview. "They've lost faith in the government and the legislature."

After receiving death threats from militias, al-Amin resigned from his seat in parliament and went back into exile in London. In meetings, American officials told him they feared that Libya was becoming a base for terrorist groups.

"They are really getting worried," al-Amin said. "But again they don't really seem to have a clue how to go about it."

In November 2013, hundreds of demonstrators chanting "We don't want armed militia" surrounded one militia headquarters in Tripoli and demanded that the group leave the city. A member of the militia opened fire on protesters with an antiaircraft gun. Demonstrators fled and returned with weapons of their own. Forty-five people died in subsequent clashes.

Days later, Pentagon officials said they had agreed to a five-month old request from Libya's beleaguered prime minister for security force training. American Special Forces soldiers would train five thousand to eight thousand Libyan government soldiers, a small fraction of the number needed in a country of six million people. American officials said the training would take place on a military base in Bulgaria. The lesson of "law and order first" remained unlearned.

CHAPTER 8

Post-Mubarak

W hile the administration could arguably take a hands-off approach in Libya, it had no such choice in Egypt. The Middle East's largest nation and its political and cultural bellwether, Egypt was a vital counterterrorism partner for the United States, a key interlocutor in the region, and a cornerstone of Israel's security. No other Western nation had as much influence in Cairo as the United States. Since the 1978 signing of the Camp David Accords, Washington had provided a staggering $40 billion in military aid and $28 billion in civilian assistance to Egypt. The only nation to receive more American aid was Israel itself.

The arrival of the Arab Spring on the streets of Cairo was a crucible for the Obama administration. In some ways, the president was doomed to fail no matter how he responded. Thirty years of American support for the authoritarian rule of Hosni Mubarak had sown deep anti-Americanism in Egyptian society. Mubarak's rule had created bitter divisions within Egypt itself. And no American policy, no matter how well executed, could stabilize Egypt without the support of Egyptians themselves.

But the administration's response to historic unrest in Egypt and other countries was muddled and inconsistent. Whatever the United States said was likely to be unpopular, but the Obama administration's lack of a clear message and strategy exacerbated animosity toward Washington.

The administration faced its first test in Egypt on January 25, 2011. Inspired by the ousting of Tunisia's president two weeks earlier, tens of thousands of Egyptians gathered in Cairo's Tahrir Square and demanded that Mubarak leave office. Over the next several days, hundreds of thousands of Egyptians joined the protests as they spread from Cairo to cities spanning the country. In an effort to thwart the opposition's ability to organize, Mubarak shut down cell phone and Internet access nationwide. The protests continued to grow.

In a speech to the nation on January 28, Mubarak announced that he was firing his current government, appointing new ministers, and enacting democratic reforms. But the Egyptian president was emphatic that he would remain in office.

After the speech, Obama called Mubarak and told him he had to take concrete steps that showed real political change in the country. Obama also made a brief statement in Washington. Trying to strike a middle ground, he urged demonstrators to protest peacefully and called on the Mubarak government to respect protesters' rights to free speech.

"There will be difficult days to come," Obama said. "But the United States will continue to stand up for the rights of the Egyptian people and work with their government in pursuit of a future that is more just, more free, and more hopeful."

On the streets of Egypt, Obama's careful stance backfired. Protesters thought his comments signaled that Washington was continuing to support Mubarak. At the same time, Mubarak loyalists were increasingly convinced the United States was secretly fomenting the antigovernment protests. Across the region, Washington was still perceived as all-powerful, despite its debacles in Iraq and Afghanistan.

Three days after Mubarak's speech, the administration dispatched Frank Wisner, a retired American diplomat with a close personal relationship with Mubarak, to meet with the Egyptian leader in Cairo. In private, Wisner conveyed a message from Obama: neither Mubarak nor his son Gamal should run in the presidential elections scheduled for September.

The following day, February 1, Mubarak made a ten-minute speech to the nation, stating that he would not run for president in September. But he also vowed to stay in office to "ensure a peaceful transfer of power," a statement that infuriated demonstrators.

A frustrated Obama called the Egyptian leader an hour after the speech. He felt Mubarak had not gone far enough.

"It is time to present to the people of Egypt its next government," Obama said, according to an account of the conversation White House officials gave to American news outlets. "The future of your country is at stake."

Mubarak replied, "Let's talk in the next three or four days," according to White House officials, adding, "and when we talk, you will find that I was right." The two men never spoke again.

The following day, groups of armed Mubarak supporters clashed with protesters in Cairo and other cities. Many of the pro-government groups were believed to include plainclothes police officers and intelligence operatives. In some cases, security forces opened fire on protesters.

As Mubarak's response to the protests grew increasingly brutal, the Obama administration's public messaging became muddled. Speaking at a security conference in Europe on February 4, Wisner, Obama's private envoy, said that Mubarak "must stay in office" in order to oversee the transition. And at the same conference, Secretary of State Clinton said that an orderly transition "takes time."

The comments angered Obama, as well as the demonstrators, who saw them as more evidence of secret American support for Mubarak. The following day, the president broke publicly with Mubarak.

"He needs to listen to what's being voiced by the Egyptian people," Obama said at a White House press conference. "And make a judgment about a pathway forward that is orderly, but that is meaningful and serious."

A week later, Mubarak resigned. All told, eight hundred people had been killed in three weeks of violence. In Egypt and across the region, radically different perceptions of Obama had taken hold. Young protesters and other supporters of the uprisings felt that he had waited too long to break with Mubarak. Saudi and Israeli officials felt that he had abandoned Mubarak too quickly and sparked instability across the region.

The same dynamic would occur again and again in the months ahead as the White House struggled to develop a coherent response to the turmoil. No "Obama doctrine" would emerge.

A month after Mubarak's fall, Obama and his foreign policy team were tested in Bahrain. Inspired by uprisings in Tunisia and Egypt, Shiite Muslims, who made up the majority of the population in the tiny Persian Gulf nation, began demanding basic rights from the country's Sunni monarch, King Hamad bin Isa al-Khalifa.

On February 14, soldiers and police killed seven demonstrators in an effort to break up the protests in the island nation of 1.2 million. As the protests continued, Shiite demonstrators broadened their demands—from the creation of a constitutional monarchy to the complete elimination of the monarchy itself.

The king and the royal families of Saudi Arabia and the United Arab Emirates dismissed the demonstrations. The Sunni monarchs viewed the protests as an effort by Shiite-dominated Iran to extend its influence into the Persian Gulf.

On March 14, twelve hundred soldiers from Saudi Arabia and eight hundred from the United Arab Emirates entered Bahrain at the request of the country's Sunni ruler. The following day, King Hamad declared martial law and a three-month state of emergency. He also ordered troops and riot police to drive protesters out of a square they had occupied in the center of the country's capital.

In Washington, the administration adopted a different stance than it had toward Egypt, where it had demanded Mubarak leave, and Libya, where it was preparing at the time to bomb Qaddafi's forces. American officials said they supported political reforms in Bahrain, but they did not call for the king to relinquish power.

White House spokesman Jay Carney was careful not to directly criticize the Saudi troop deployment in Bahrain. He said the White House felt it was "not an invasion" of the country and called for "restraint" and "political dialogue" from all sides.

Inside the administration, there was deep division over how to respond to the Arab Spring. In one camp, some younger White House officials, including Ben Rhodes, the president's foreign policy speechwriter, and Susan Rice, the U.S. ambassador to the UN, worried that Obama could end up on the wrong side of history if he failed to support the protests. In the other camp, Clinton, Defense Secretary Gates, and White House counterterrorism adviser John Brennan warned that American alliances with Saudi Arabia and other regimes in the region were important in the fight against terrorism.

Ultimately, the threat of an empowered Iran prompted the administration to side with the Sunni monarchy and its Saudi backers. A close ally and the headquarters of the U.S. Navy's Fifth Fleet, Bahrain had served as a counterweight to Iran for decades. Fearing that the toppling of Bahrain's monarchy would aid Tehran, the administration said little as the small Persian Gulf nation crushed dissent.

* * *

A similar dynamic emerged in Yemen. The administration's fears of strengthening a strategic rival—al-Qaeda—prompted a more muted response than in Egypt and Libya. After demonstrators in Tunisia ousted that nation's leader in mid-January 2011, student-led protests began in Yemen. The fall of Mubarak in mid-February 2011 boosted the size of the protests.

The poorest country in the Arab world, Yemen had been ruled by President Ali Abdullah Saleh for thirty-two years. In a country of 24 million, 40 percent of the population lived on two dollars or less a day. A third faced food shortages. Across the country, an affiliate of al-Qaeda, a southern separatist movement, and Shia insurgents in the north known as the Houthis all challenged Saleh's rule.

Saleh was a mercurial but generally cooperative partner in the American effort to counter al-Qaeda. He received weaponry from the United States and allowed the U.S. military and CIA to carry out drone strikes in the country. But he declined other, unspecified American requests.

WikiLeaks cables described by the *New York Times* said that Saleh told the commander of U.S. forces in the Middle East, General David Petraeus, that drone strikes could continue as long as the Yemeni officials could falsely claim they were conducting the strikes themselves.

"We'll continue saying the bombs are ours, not yours," Saleh said, according to a cable.

In another meeting, Saleh complained to the State Department's counterterrorism chief, Daniel Benjamin, that the United States was unreliable. Americans were "hot-blooded and hasty when you need us," he said, but "cold-blooded and British when we need you."

As protests spread across Yemen in February, the Obama administration privately maintained its support of Saleh and refrained from criticizing him in public. On March 18, unidentified gunmen fired on a protest in the capital, Sanaa, killing more than fifty people. The following week, a wave of senior government and military officials joined the opposition.

In late March, American officials determined that opposition to Saleh was negatively impacting American counterterrorism operations. The administration decided the longtime ruler was unlikely to meet opposition demands and should be eased out of power.

An administration official told the *New York Times* that the standoff between the president and the protesters was aiding extremists. "Groups of various stripes—al-Qaeda, Houthis, tribal elements, and secessionists," the official said, "are exploiting the current political turbulence and emerging fissures within the military and security services for their own gain."

As in Egypt, the administration's delayed backing of the protests exasperated demonstrators. The United States was again accused of having a double standard.

"We are really very, very angry because America until now didn't help us similar to what Mr. Obama said that Mubarak has to leave now," Tawakkol Karman, a leader of the antigovernment youth movement and winner of the 2011 Nobel Peace Prize, told the *Times*. "Obama says he appreciated the courage and dignity of Tunisian people. He didn't say that for Yemeni people."

Saleh, meanwhile, resisted American calls to give up power. The administration's shifting position alienated both sides in a bitterly divided Yemen. After narrowly surviving an assassination attempt, Saleh transferred power to his deputy in 2012. Across the region, the United States was widely viewed as backing autocrats, not democracy.

As the Arab Spring progressed, the level of violence rose and the euphoria that had greeted the toppling of autocrats in Tunisia and Egypt faded. In April, President Bashar al-Assad of Syria responded to peaceful protests with more brutality than any other leader, killing 280 protesters in six weeks. As Tunisia and Egypt embarked on tenuous transitions, governments in Syria, Libya, Yemen, and Bahrain violently suppressed their opponents.

On May 19, 2011, Obama delivered a speech at the State Department designed to clarify America's stance on the Arab Spring. In an ambitious forty-five-minute address, the president praised the uprisings and argued that America should remain engaged in the region.

"Our own future is bound to this region by the forces of economics and security, by history and by faith," he said at the outset. "Today, I want to talk about this change—the forces that are driving it and how we can respond in a way that advances our values and strengthens our security."

Obama praised the ordinary citizens who participated in the Arab uprisings, comparing them with the American colonists who carried out the Boston Tea Party and civil rights leader Rosa Parks. He reiterated the theme of his 2009 speech in Cairo.

"And that's why, two years ago in Cairo, I began to broaden our engagement based upon mutual interests and mutual respect," he said. "I believed then—and I believe now—that we have a stake not just in the stability of nations, but in the self-determination of individuals."

"The status quo is not sustainable," Obama added. "Societies held together by fear and repression may offer the illusion of stability for a time, but they are built upon fault lines that will eventually tear asunder."

Vowing to "show that America values the dignity of the street vendor in Tunisia more than the raw power of the dictator," Obama said the United States would support democratic change. "After decades of accepting the world as it is in the region, we have a chance to pursue the world as it should be."

Tempering his remarks, the former constitutional law professor cautioned that the United States should be wary of Bush-style overreach. "We must proceed with a sense of humility," Obama said. "It's not America that put people into the streets of Tunis or Cairo—it was the people themselves who launched these movements, and it's the people themselves that must ultimately determine their outcome."

The president then listed three principles the United States would "speak out for" in the Middle East. "The United States opposes the use of violence and repression against the people of the region," he said. "The United States supports a set of universal rights. And these rights include free speech, the freedom of peaceful assembly, the freedom of religion, equality for men and women under the rule of law, and the right to choose your own leaders—whether you live in Baghdad or Damascus, Sanaa or Tehran. And we support political and economic reform in the Middle East and North Africa," he added, "that can meet the legitimate aspirations of ordinary people throughout the region."

Obama went on to harshly criticize the violent crackdowns in Libya, Syria, Yemen, and Bahrain. He called for an Israel-Palestinian peace settlement based on Israel's 1967 borders, a stance opposed by Israeli prime minister Benjamin Netanyahu. And he proposed a series of economic steps to aid the region.

The administration would apply the successful reforms that had aided post-Communist Eastern Europe to the post–Arab Spring, he said: creating enterprise funds, $2 billion in loan guarantees for U.S. businesses investing in the region, and European Union–like incentives that would grant beneficial trade terms to nations that enacted political and economic reform.

"Just as EU membership served as an incentive for reform in Europe," Obama said, "so should the vision of a modern and prosperous economy create a powerful force for reform in the Middle East and North Africa."

The president also announced that the United States was forgiving $1 billion of Egypt's debt and guaranteeing another $1 billion in borrowing for infrastructure projects.

Reactions to the speech were mixed. American commentators pointed out that the economic components were minuscule compared with the post–World War II Marshall Plan and post-1989 U.S. efforts in the former Soviet bloc. Supporters of Israel said Obama had undermined an ally. And in the Arab world, many young people still viewed him as slow to abandon Mubarak and his brethren. They doubted the United States would move beyond its traditional approach of supporting Saudi Arabia, Israel, and autocrats.

Anthony Haddad, a twenty-five-year-old student in Beirut, predicted that nothing would change. "Obama's rhetoric won't consistently be met with action," he told the *Los Angeles Times*.

Exceptions existed, such as the NATO intervention in Libya, but Haddad's skepticism was generally justified. Over the next eighteen months, Obama distanced himself from the democratic change he had embraced in the speech. His administration was also slow to implement the economic initiatives he had promised.

In Obama's defense, key leaders in the region, such as Egyptian president Mohammed Morsi, Turkish Prime Minister Tayyep Erdogan, and some members of the Syrian opposition, performed abysmally and squandered historic opportunities. They embraced an illiberal, winner-take-all style of majority-rule democracy, centralizing power at every turn, and refusing to compromise.

And three dynamics at home limited Obama's ability to respond: the president's tight 2012 reelection race, Washington's deep fiscal problems, and the widespread sense among Americans that the United States had achieved nothing in Iraq and Afghanistan. Skepticism among voters regarding any major new American venture in the region was widespread.

In many ways, Hillary Clinton's tenure as secretary of state illustrated the limits of diplomacy in an age of post–Iraq and Afghanistan isolationism. It also showed the controlling nature of the Obama White House. When Obama recruited her to serve as secretary of state, he famously agreed to Clinton's demand that she be able to fill all political appointees at the State Department with her own people. But suspicions between the two leaders' staffs from the 2008 campaign lingered, according to aides to both. During her first years in office, Clinton's freedom to maneuver was limited.

Accelerating a trend that has existed since John F. Kennedy was president, the Obama administration centralized foreign policy decision making in the White House. Clinton was free to pursue economic development, women's rights, high-tech diplomacy, and a handful of other issues. But the White House maintained viselike control of foreign policy issues that might impact Obama's reelection chances. In a 2014 memoir, former Defense Secretary Gates wrote that the Obama "White House was by far the most centralized and controlling in national security of any I had seen since Richard Nixon and Henry Kissinger ruled the roost."

Using phrases like "smart power" and "leading through civilian power," Clinton tried to elevate the role of the State Department and diplomacy, aid, and economics in national security. Creating a quadrennial strategic review process that mirrored a similar Pentagon review, she reorganized the department and created two new bureaus: one focusing on economic growth, energy, and the environment and the other on civilian security, democracy, and human rights.

She also tried to get the hidebound diplomats to embrace "economic statecraft" as part of their mission. "Right now, the challenges of a changing world and the needs of the American people demand that our foreign policy community, as the late Steve Jobs put it, 'think different,'" Clinton said in a 2011 speech. "That is why I have put what I call economic statecraft at the heart of our foreign policy agenda."

Clinton said economic statecraft involved two goals: promoting

American exports as a way to create jobs at home, and harnessing economic power, growth, and change to strengthen U.S. influence abroad.

In an effort to strengthen the department and decrease its dependence on contractors, Clinton hired 1,700 new Foreign Service staff in 2009 and 2010, increasing the size of the department by 17 percent. Arguing that the State Department and foreign aid represented only one percent of the overall federal budget, she set a goal of increasing the department's staff by 25 percent by 2013. As a candidate in 2008, Obama had vowed to double U.S. foreign aid.

Washington's fiscal problems ended those plans. The sequester and other budget cuts dramatically slowed spending and hiring in 2011 and 2012. The target date for increasing the size of the department by 25 percent was pushed back a decade—from 2013 to 2023, rendering it effectively meaningless.

Finally, in the policy arena, Clinton proposed that the United States carry out a "pivot to Asia" after spending vast amounts of lives and treasure in Iraq and Afghanistan. The goal was to shift the focus of American foreign policy from the Middle East to the part of the world with the fastest-growing economies and largest potential markets for U.S. goods.

Obama, National Security Adviser Tom Donilon, and other White House officials strongly supported the initiative. In an interview, Rhodes, Obama's main foreign policy speechwriter, said reducing the U.S. role in the Middle East remained a core administration goal, "fundamentally changing the way the United States is present in Asia, Africa, and Latin America," he told me. "So that the way the U.S. is positioned in the world lines up with what we're going to care about in the world in ten years."

But Obama, Clinton, and the rest of the administration found themselves repeatedly pulled back into the Middle East. After Muslim

Brotherhood leader Morsi was elected President of Egypt in June 2012, Clinton visited Cairo and saw the country's growing political polarization and anti-Americanism firsthand.

As she exited the recently reopened American consulate in Alexandria, anti-Morsi demonstrators hurled shoes and tomatoes at her car and shouted "Monica," a reference to Monica Lewinsky. They were convinced that Clinton and other American officials had surreptitiously fixed Egypt's presidential elections so that the Brotherhood would win.

At the same time, Syria devolved into sectarian civil war. Displaying astonishing brutality, Assad's Alawite-dominated security forces fired on unarmed demonstrators, fired Scud missiles into cities, and dropped enormous homemade barrel bombs from helicopters. The Sunni-dominated opposition formed militias but were clearly outgunned.

In the summer of 2012, Clinton and then-CIA director David Petraeus secretly proposed to Obama that the United States begin covertly arming moderate elements of the Syrian opposition. Defense Secretary Leon Panetta and Chairman of the Joint Chiefs of Staff Martin Dempsey supported the plan as well.

Obama had publicly said that Assad must go, but he was locked in a tight reelection campaign. The president rejected the covert plan but did not tone down his public rhetoric. In a remark that would come back to haunt him, Obama said in an August 2012 press conference that Assad would cross a "red line" if he used chemical weapons in Syria.

A month later, Libya put Clinton's performance under a microscope as well. On September 11, 2012, militants attacked the U.S. consulate in Benghazi and a nearby CIA annex, killing Ambassador Chris Stevens and three other Americans. The deaths were the largest single failure of Clinton's tenure and set off a political firestorm in Washington.

Republicans accused Clinton of ignoring pleas for additional security guards and other resources in Benghazi. Democrats complained that House Republicans had cut $340 million in funding from the department's request for embassy security.

State Department officials told me that both sides were missing a central lesson of Benghazi: an excess of in-house bureaucracy and a lack of government capacity. After the Libyan government barred American security contractors from operating in the country, the State Department did not have enough government security staff to properly defend the consulate.

An Accountability Review Board found that department bureaucrats in Washington had turned down repeated requests for additional security personnel in Benghazi. Years of struggling to obtain resources "conditioned a few State Department managers to favor restricting the use of resources as a general orientation." Ignoring pleas from the field, the institution's sclerotic mid-level management had failed Stevens and his colleagues.

"Systemic failures and leadership and management deficiencies at senior levels within two bureaus of the State Department," the board found, "resulted in a Special Mission security posture that was inadequate for Benghazi and grossly inadequate to deal with the attack that took place."

The board called for the department to be bolder, nimbler, and better resourced.

"It is imperative for the State Department to be mission-driven, rather than resource-constrained," it said, "particularly when being present in increasingly risky areas of the world is integral to U.S. national security."

Obama won reelection and John Kerry, a former senator with a lifelong interest in the Middle East, became his new secretary of state. But the president's challenges in the region only grew.

An activist secretary of state, Kerry immediately plunged into Middle Eastern diplomacy. Whereas Clinton had limited her risk taking in the region, presumably to protect a potential future presidential run, Kerry had nothing to lose. His 2004 defeat at the hands of George W. Bush had ended his dream of becoming president.

Traveling at a faster rate than Clinton in his first year, Kerry set out three ambitious goals: reviving the Israeli-Palestinian peace process, striking a nuclear deal with Iran, and bringing peace to Syria.

Scoffed at by many experts, Kerry made frequent gaffes and was accused of being primarily driven by ego. But he surprised observers when he convinced Israeli and Palestinian officials to begin nine months of peace negotiations in August 2013. The talks were widely expected to fail, but simply getting the two sides back to the table briefly boosted Kerry's credibility.

His influence in other foreign policy areas was limited. As Clinton had experienced, the White House retained sweeping control of U.S. policy in Syria and Iran.

Syria, more than any issue, bedeviled Obama and his White House aides. Over the course of 2013, the death toll from the conflict soared to 100,000, and 2.3 million Syrian refugees fled to Turkey, Lebanon, and Jordan. As sectarian tensions spread, fears of a regional war grew.

A key element of Obama's strategy in Syria—relying on regional allies—failed completely. In an effort to limit direct American involvement and avoid the mistakes of George W. Bush, Obama tried to work through nations in the region. Turkey, Qatar, and Saudi Arabia pledged to strengthen the Syrian opposition politically and militarily. Instead, the countries backed their own factions in the opposition, which fueled division and deadlock.

In 2013, jihadists flooded into Syria and filled the leadership vacuum. With Saudi intelligence officials and wealthy individuals in the Persian Gulf bankrolling them, their bravery, weaponry, and cash prompted young Syrians to join them. The jihadist hijacking of the opposition was a disaster for the United States.

A steady stream of news reports described to Americans how the Syrian opposition was now allied with al Qaeda. One of Assad's key propaganda claims—that he was battling jihadists—had become a reality. The American public's already minuscule interest in supporting the rebels evaporated.

While the United States and its regional allies squabbled, Russia and Iran decisively supported Assad. Using its United Nations Security Council veto, Russia blocked repeated attempts by the United States and other nations to pass Security Council resolutions authorizing the use of force against the Syrian regime.

Moscow also sold sophisticated weaponry to Assad, and Tehran sent planeloads of fighters, weapons, and cash to Damascus. In the spring of 2013, thousands of Hezbollah fighters, Iran's Lebanese proxies, arrived in Syria to fight alongside Assad's forces. Syrian government soldiers and Hezbollah fighters took control of the strategic town of Qusayr. For the first time in two years, Assad had gained the military upper hand.

Assad also called Obama's bluff regarding the use of chemical weapons. In a series of small-scale attacks, Assad's forces gassed opposition over the course of the spring. European intelligence agencies publicly announced that chemical weapons had been used, but the Obama administration said it was investigating the attacks.

After steadfastly resisting any direct involvement in the war for two years, Obama made a split-the-difference decision in April 2013. He secretly authorized a covert plan to arm Syria's rebels. In truth, the effort was meager and slow moving. For the next two months, no arms reached the rebels.

* * *

In July, Obama made another split-the-difference decision. After millions of anti–Muslim Brotherhood protesters took to the streets to demand that President Morsi resign, the Egyptian military toppled him in a coup.

Over the next several weeks, the Egyptian army and security forces killed a thousand Brotherhood members, many of them unarmed demonstrators, and wounded and jailed thousands more. On August 14, more than six hundred demonstrators died when Egyptian police stormed two Brotherhood protest camps. The crushing of the Brotherhood was now bloodier than the Mubarak crackdown that prompted Obama to personally call for the Egyptian leader to resign in 2011.

In an August 15 statement from Martha's Vineyard, where Obama was on vacation, the president said he was canceling a biannual joint military exercise, but he declined to call the removal of Morsi a coup. Under American law, that designation would automatically trigger the cutoff of $1.3 billion in U.S. military aid to Egypt. In a confusing final passage, Obama said the United States would maintain its relationship with Egypt's new leaders but also support democratic ideals.

"Our partnership must also advance the principles that we believe in and that so many Egyptians have sacrificed for these last several years, no matter what party or faction they belong to," he said. "So America will work with all those in Egypt and around the world who support a future of stability that rests on a foundation of justice and peace and dignity."

After making the statement, Obama went golfing. Eight weeks later, after an internal administration review, the State Department announced that the United States was suspending $260 million of the $1.2 billion in American aid. Equipment that helped Egyptian army efforts to prevent Sinai-based militants from attacking Israel would continue to be delivered. Obama made no public comment.

* * *

Finally, at the end of a summer that seemed to extinguish all of the promise of the Arab Spring, an August 21 sarin gas attack in a Damascus suburb forced Obama's hand. As amateur videos of children gasping for air and hundreds of corpses emerged, Obama told his aides he was prepared to launch air strikes against Assad's forces to enforce his "red line." But after the British Parliament voted against strikes, Obama decided to seek a vote of support from the U.S. Congress.

As congressional and public opposition to strikes mounted, Obama tried to lay out, yet again, a vision of America's role in the world, in an address to the American public. But he contradicted himself.

"America is not the world's policeman," he said. "Terrible things happen across the globe, and it is beyond our means to right every wrong. But when, with modest effort and risk, we can stop children from being gassed to death, and thereby make our own children safer over the long run, I believe we should act.

"That's what makes America different," Obama added. "That's what makes us exceptional. With humility, but with resolve, let us never lose sight of that essential truth."

In the end, a Russian proposal to have international inspectors remove Assad's chemical weapons from Syria gave Obama a way out. Four days after the president's speech, Kerry and Russian foreign minister Sergey Lavrov struck an agreement that required the Syrian government to hand over its chemical weapons. Obama's policy had quietly shifted from "Assad must go" to "Assad's chemical weapons must go." The Syrian leader had survived to fight another day. And he was free to crush his opponents with conventional weapons.

In September 2013, a beleaguered Obama addressed the United Nations General Assembly. Four years after his "new beginning" speech in Cairo and two years after his "universal rights" speech at the State Department, the president tried to again articulate his administration's priorities in the Middle East.

Obama stated that the United States would "use all elements of our power, including military force" to secure four "core interests" in the region. He vowed to "confront external aggression" against U.S. allies, "ensure the free flow of energy," dismantle terrorist networks that "threaten our people," and "not tolerate the development or use of weapons of mass destruction."

Obama said the United States would pursue two diplomatic goals in the Middle East: securing an Israeli-Palestinian peace settlement, and an agreement to prevent Iran from acquiring a nuclear weapon.

The four "core interests" and two diplomatic initiatives Obama described are sound policy. But his administration's repeated declarations that it will not use force in the region undermine those goals. The credible threat of force is an important diplomatic tool.

Looking back, Obama's inconsistent case-by-case response to the Arab Spring failed him. The White House quickly embraced protesters in Tunisia, gradually called for Mubarak's ouster in Egypt and then turned a blind eye toward brutal military crackdowns in Bahrain and Egypt. In Yemen, it changed course midway. In Syria, it called for Assad's ouster and then backed down.

No American policy could have stabilized the region. But the administration's inconsistent rhetoric complicated its response to a historic moment, stoking anger and confusion across the region. The United States was always likely to be loathed in the post–Arab Spring Middle East, but the administration's vacillation exacerbated that hatred and served American foreign policy poorly.

CHAPTER 9

Little Washington

O ne American who believed Obama would revitalize the State Department was Steven R. Koltai. A fifty-five-year-old former Warner Brothers executive and Internet entrepreneur, Koltai had watched Obama's 2009 speech calling for a "new beginning" between the United States and the Islamic world from his vacation home in Maine. Obama's vow to host a Summit on Entrepreneurship between American and Muslim business leaders thrilled and inspired him.

The State Department had recently accepted Koltai as a Franklin Fellow, a new Obama administration initiative designed to bring private sector and academic experts to work at the State Department and USAID for a year. On paper, the program was an innovative attempt to help the government marshal the expertise of American business and academia. But in reality it was a marginal effort that was no match for the State Department's entrenched bureaucracy and risk aversion.

The fellowship was unpaid and did not offer fellows a housing stipend. Instead, the State Department asked that businesses and academic institutions pay fellows salaries during their year in Washington. After thirty years in the private sector, Koltai was wealthy enough that he didn't need a salary, but he was deeply skeptical of government in general. Obama's embrace of entrepreneurship, though, convinced him to give public service a chance.

"This is my life's work," Koltai later said, referring to promoting entrepreneurship. "The United States has not put what I consider the central strand of our DNA into the service of our foreign policy."

Bald, bearish, and intensely driven, Koltai was born in Hungary. He and his family fled the country when he was a toddler during the 1956 Hungarian Revolution. The child of an academic, he grew up in Los Angeles and Kansas City, Missouri, and received a bachelor's degree from Tufts University in 1976 and a master's degree from Tuft's Fletcher School of Law and Diplomacy in 1978.

Most of his classmates chose to become diplomats and bankers. Koltai, a fluent Hungarian and French speaker, became a businessman and consultant with a blue-chip résumé. In the 1980s, he worked at McKinsey & Company, Salomon Brothers, and cofounded a firm that would become SES/Astra, one of Europe's largest satellite television companies. Returning to Los Angeles in 1987, he married, had two sons, and worked as a senior executive at Warner Brothers for nine years.

In the late 1990s, he rode the tech bubble—and bust. In 1996, Koltai founded Event411, an online event registration and management company that provided the software for the 2000 Los Angeles Democratic National Convention, the 2000 Salt Lake City Winter Olympics, and corporate clients. After the dot-com bubble burst and the 9/11 attacks decimated the convention business, the firm went out of business in 2002.

Over the next several years, Koltai ran his own consulting and investment company, advised Lifetime Television, served on various boards at Tufts, and helped the school develop an entrepreneurial leadership program. In August 2009, he arrived for his first day of work at the State Department. Over the next two years, his own small attempt to bring change to the organization would fail.

First Koltai hurled himself into turning Obama's promise of hosting a summit for entrepreneurs into reality. His mentor and boss was Lorraine Hariton, the State Department's special representative for commercial and business affairs. A successful Silicon Valley executive, Hariton, like Richard Holbrooke, was one of a handful of "special representatives" Clinton had appointed to address the country's most pressing foreign policy issues—Afghanistan-Pakistan, Israel-Palestine, and dismally low American exports.

The entrepreneurship initiative was part of Clinton's effort to introduce "economic statecraft" to the State Department. She and her aides argued that promoting entrepreneurship would help create jobs and foster political stability in the Middle East. Koltai spent his first three months working as the lead organizer of Obama's promised Presidential Summit on Entrepreneurship. Held in April 2010, it brought 220 entrepreneurs from 55 Muslim communities to Washington.

Koltai then helped launch the Global Entrepreneurship Program, a seemingly model public-private partnership that included Cisco, Ernst & Young, and Google from the private sector; MIT, Babson College, and the American University in Cairo from academia; and Endeavor and TechnoServ from the nonprofit world. USAID, the Overseas Private Investment Corporation, the Small Business Administration, and the Commerce Department participated as well.

The program opened offices in Egypt, Indonesia, and Turkey, where "lead entrepreneurs" operated programs that gave local entrepreneurs mentoring, training, and contact with American angel investors. Koltai and others led "entrepreneurship delegations" that brought successful start-up executives, angel investors, and business school professors to Lebanon, Jordan, Egypt, and Indonesia.

But Koltai struggled to get long-term funding for the program. He temporarily cobbled together $1.5 million from various initiatives but never secured permanent funding—or staffers—for it. His argument that entrepreneurship training was a more cost-effective form of development failed to win over skeptics.

"The kind of program I'm talking about—for the world, it's $100 million," he said.

Members of Congress were more comfortable funding experimental weapons and surveillance systems than untested forms of economic engagement. And State Department officials were more interested in traditional diplomacy.

Koltai found government workers underpaid, discouraged and cynical. They "yawned" at the announcement of new presidential initiatives, according to Koltai, dismissing the programs as political theatrics or changes that the next administration would reverse in four years. Instead of rushing to carry out the president's orders, some State Department staffers did just enough to not endanger their jobs. Others, he found, were committed to government service but beaten down by a system that resisted changed.

"There are an incredible number of really smart, really dedicated people who are incredibly frustrated," he said.

Fearful of criticism and budget cuts from Capitol Hill, risk aversion was endemic across the government, according to Koltai and other former government officials who had worked in the private sector. In business, taking risks and failing was expected. In government, members of Congress and the news media lampooned the smallest mistake.

"I was able to generate zero dollars of funding and zero FTEs," Koltai said, using the term for full-time-equivalent employees. "What we were able to do was write speeches."

One midlevel administration official who worked in the venture capital field before taking a post in the Obama administration said the public system was paralyzed. In venture capital, he said, as many as eighteen out of twenty investments lose money, but the goal is to learn from one's mistakes. In Washington, a single failure can doom a career.

"It's very hard to innovate and to learn in these programs," said the official, who asked not to be named. "If you fail once, you get screwed." The result was an extraordinarily cautious and territorial system that infuriated Koltai. Government workers, meanwhile, found him grating.

"He was a one-man show," recalled a government official who worked with Koltai and also asked not to be named. "To succeed in Washington, you have to be a team player and bring people along with you."

What angered Koltai the most was the department's reliance on contractors. While government bureaucrats fretted over evaporating slots, funding, and authority, contractors overflowed with resources. As a business executive, Koltai was astonished by how the contracting system worked.

Based on the numbers he saw while in government and his own experience running businesses, he estimated that State Department contractors regularly made a 30 percent profit while performing poorly and facing little competition. He watched cautious and overworked government contracting officers choose the same firm year after year because doing so allowed them to avoid congressional or media scrutiny.

"The only way to not make a mistake is to do nothing," Koltai said. "And the only way to not choose the wrong contractor is to choose the one you're already using."

After the fall of Mubarak, Koltai tried to convince USAID to revamp a $34 million program that had been created in 2008 to "improve the business environment" in Egypt. With more freedom to operate in the country, he hoped to divert some of the money to training young Egyptian technology entrepreneurs and exposing them to American executives and investors.

But the contractor—Chemonics—the same company that had hired Chuck Grader years earlier in southern Afghanistan—refused to change the program. When the USAID procurement officer handling the contract challenged Chemonics, he found himself outnumbered. Citing language in its contract, the company threatened to go to court over the issue. The system astounded Koltai.

"Chemonics has a whole legal department whose existence is based on memorizing the fine print," he said. "The person overseeing the public money is outgunned. We, the American taxpayer, did not have the right to say 'stop the presses, there's been a revolution.'"

The USAID procurement officer impressed him. He declined to name him but said he was a "smart, dedicated" civil servant, with relatively low pay, scant support, and tough working conditions.

"He was paid eighty-five thousand dollars while managing hundreds of thousands of dollars," Koltai said. "You'd never find that in the private sector."

After his one-year fellowship ended, he was hired by the State Department to continue on as a senior adviser for entrepreneurship. After two years, he left in frustration. The depth of Washington's polarization depressed Koltai. Business was not inherently evil, as the Far Left contended. And government was not inherently a menace, as the Far Right contended. Koltai believed that Silicon Valley and other successful entrepreneurial "ecosystems" were the product of public and private partnerships. Together, federally funded research universities and ruthlessly capitalistic venture capital firms created innovation.

"There is no example of a successful entrepreneurial system that did not have the government in the lead," Koltai said. "You don't just start a venture fund. You don't just do training. You do a basket of things."

But implementing new initiatives proved extraordinarily difficult. The byzantine federal procurement process minimized risk—the opposite of the venture capital system—and blocked change.

"The number one problem in connecting the dots is the procurement process," he said. "In my view, the key to changing that is on the Hill."

Until the president and Congress revamp civilian agencies, implementing dynamic policies will be difficult.

"If the axle of the car is broken," he said, "whether Mario Andretti or you gets behind the wheel, you're not going to be able to drive it."

The stagnation in the State Department is a reflection of a broader, long-term shift of money, talent, and authority from the public sector to the private sector under the Reagan, Bush, and Clinton administrations. As government contracting exploded in Washington during the 1990s and 2000s, Wall Street firms—smelling a profit—arrived in force.

The first private equity firm to move into government contracting was the Carlyle Group. In 1989, David M. Rubenstein, a lawyer and former domestic policy adviser to President Jimmy Carter, cofounded the firm with William E. Conway Jr., a former MCI executive, and Daniel A. D'Aniello, a corporate executive. Over the course of the 1990s, Carlyle bought up defense and aerospace companies and quickly became the leading private equity investor in the sector.

The driving force behind the strategy was Frank Carlucci, a former Reagan administration national security adviser and defense secretary. A college roommate of Donald Rumsfeld at Princeton and former CIA operative, Carlucci served as the Carlyle Group's chairman from 1992 to 2003.

James Baker III, former secretary of state, served as the group's senior counselor, and its advisers and executives included former President George H. W. Bush, former Clinton White House Chief of Staff Thomas "Mack" McLarty, former Securities and Exchange Commission Chairman Arthur Levitt, former British Prime Minister John Major, and former Philippines President Fidel Ramos. A half-brother of Osama bin Laden who was estranged from the al-Qaeda leader invested in Carlyle in the 1990s. He withdrew the funds after the 9/11 attacks.

Carlyle profited from the invasions of Afghanistan and Iraq by cashing out at the right time. Its largest defense investment was the 1997 purchase of United Defense Industries—which makes artillery, missiles, and other weapons systems. As the Iraq war raged in 2004, Carlyle sold the company to the British defense conglomerate BAE at a profit of $1 billion. In 2008, Carlyle purchased government contractor Booz Allen Hamilton for $2.5 billion. In 2012, Booz Allen received $3.8 billion in federal contracts, much of it for work with the CIA, and was the eighth-largest federal contractor.

Today, Carlyle is legendary in private equity circles. Company officials say they buy poorly managed firms, revamp them, and provide better services to the government and consumers. It has $150 billion in assets, invests across the economy, and owns companies ranging from Bain Capital to Dunkin' Donuts. The firm's three founders are believed to be worth as much as $2 billion each.

DynCorp, meanwhile, is shifting back to defense contracting. In 2012, it was the the country's eleventh-largest government contractor and received $2.3 billion in federal contracts. As of November 2013, the company's owner was Cerberus Capital Management, the $20 billion New York based private equity firm headed by longtime Republican donor Stephen Feinberg. Cerberus's senior executives include former Vice President Dan Quayle and former Bush administration Treasury Secretary John Snow.

Another firm with Wall Street ties that profited handsomely while performing questionably as a post-9/11 contractor is Bearing-Point. The McLean, Virginia–based global consulting firm was hired to provide training and monitoring to the Afghan and Iraqi Ministries of Finance. Between 2001 and 2009, the firm received $1 billion in State Department contracts for its work in Afghanistan and Iraq. Auditors later found that the firm failed to report signs of the looting of up to $850 million from Afghanistan's Kabul Bank to U.S. officials. After expanding too quickly around the world, BearingPoint filed for bankruptcy in 2009.

New York–based Deloitte, the Wall Street professional services firm, bought BearingPoint's government contracting business and took over its Afghanistan operation. Auditors found that Deloitte also failed to report to U.S. officials signs that Kabul Bank was being looted. Officials from Deloitte said the firm's work in Afghanistan was "primarily advisory" and "included assistance with training programs and advising on rules and procedures" but did not involve "supervision or examination of any bank." The firm continues to receive work from the U.S. government. In 2012 Deloitte won $1.2 billion in federal contracts and was the twenty-fourth-largest government contractor in the United States.

Chemonics, the firm whose conduct in southern Afghanistan angered Chuck Grader nearly a decade ago and Steven Koltai in Egypt more recently, remains on the government payroll. Company officials continue to defend the quality of their work.

In 2006, Scott Spangler, the Republican donor and former Bush administration official who purchased Chemonics in 1999, sold his controlling interest in the firm to Eyk Van Otterloo, a founding partner of Grantham, Mayo, and Van Otterloo & Company, a Boston-based private equity firm with $104 billion in assets. In 2011, Chemonics became employee-owned but Van Otterloo remained chairman. In 2012, the firm was the fortieth-largest contractor in the United States. That year, it received $522 million in government contracts, nearly all of them from USAID. It still holds the USAID contract in Egypt, which is both vital and expected to rapidly expand.

USAID, meanwhile, continues to flounder. Between 2001 and 2010, Congress doubled the agency's budget but cut staffing by 30 percent. Some staff was added by the Obama administration, but State, White House, and congressional officials continued to lambaste its performance.

In an effort to remake its image, USAID hired Maura O'Neill as its chief innovation officer in 2010. Before serving as chief of staff for the Agriculture Department and Washington Senator Maria Cantwell, O'Neill started four companies and taught entrepreneurship at the Haas School of Business at the University of California, Berkeley. At USAID, she launched Development Innovation Ventures, a program in which the agency tries to replicate the success of the venture capital model—where the majority of investments fail—and apply it to government. Under the program, USAID invests small amounts in projects—usually less than $1 million—and quickly tests to see whether they succeed or fail. If they succeed, they are scaled up and shifted to other parts of the agency.

"Allow us to make a lot of small investments, fail fast, and scale up what works," she said in an interview.

She argued that the rise of developing economies, from China to Brazil—as well as a surge in technological advances—makes successful development more possible than ever. She and other USAID officials point to the growth of mobile phone use worldwide as an example of technology driven public-private partnerships that AID can promote.

"The developing world is more dynamic than it has ever been," O'Neill said. "Connective technologies have made more opportunities for breakthroughs."

Mark Ward, the longtime AID official who served as its head of procurement from 2006 to 2008, said the core problem was the agency's lack of staff. Congress hurls money at the agency but refuses to give it staff to manage it.

"Given that the number of Foreign Service officers has fallen so precipitously since the Vietnam War—we have one-tenth of the number we had," he said, "we have no choice but to turn to contractors to do the work."

When Ward was the head of procurement, he oversaw sixty to seventy USAID procurement officers who were expected to monitor aid programs worldwide. Under pressure to approve the dispersals of billions of dollars in assistance, Ward and his staff created enormous contracts.

"We have very few people to keep an eye on the contractors, and that naturally has led to fewer and bigger contracts," he said. "I had plenty of money but I didn't have enough people to oversee the awarding of contracts. What do you do? You award fewer contracts. The way to move the money quickly is to award megacontracts to megacontractors."

He said he shared Holbrooke's desire for smaller contracts. While the veteran diplomats were rough on the edges and at times alienated people, he had the right strategy.

"The right approach, the better approach, is bite-sized contracts and grants that are close to the action, that are more flexible, that can't respond to changed approaches," he said. "That's the thing we need."

The solution, he said, is simple.

"It all begins with doing something that is very boring and very Washington," he said. "You need to hire more contracting officers."

Shamila Chaudhary, the young Pakistani American who worked as a State Department and White House aide, resigned from her position at the National Security Council in 2011. After nearly a decade at the State Department, and the White House, she questioned Washington's commitment to long-term strategies in Afghanistan and Pakistan.

"When I left I was depressed and disappointed," she said. "I was depressed because I didn't really see an end in sight. I didn't see how we were going to improve the relations we had with both of these countries based on the timeline we had, which was very short."

She said she disagreed with some of Koltai's criticisms. The government will always function differently from the private sector, she argued because taxpayers' dollars are at stake. In the government, numerous stakeholders must be brought on board to win approval of new initiatives. In the private sector, a limited number of major investors are involved.

"The number of people you are accountable to is much less, that's why you get things done much faster," she said. "In the government, you are accountable to every American citizen. These are taxpayer dollars and people take that very seriously."

Chaudhary described the process of drafting new policies, building support for them, and implementing them as arduous.

"You have to build consensus and political will at so many levels," she said. "And when you do that you usually get something that is very watered down, something that is not really as ambitious as the first person thought."

She said the core problem was that American officials were unable to move beyond seeing Afghanistan and Pakistan as security threats to the United States, not nations. She wished a more long-term, normalized relationship could exist.

"When you actually talked about it in nonsecurity ways, people couldn't get their heads around it," she said. "It's not Pakistan for Pakistan's sake. It's not Afghanistan for Afghanistan's sake."

For understandable reasons, even though it is counterproductive in some ways, American policy makers continue to view the region through a counterterrorism prism.

"We're not able to pull ourselves out of this," she said, "because the wounds of 9/11 are still very strong."

There have been some efforts in the State Department to learn lessons from the post-9/11 decade. In 2004, the Bush administration created the Office of the Coordinator for Reconstruction and Stabilization. The initiative was an attempt to create a civilian surge capacity in the State Department, formally known as the Civilian Response Corps, made up of federal employees with experience in relief efforts, reconstruction, and training in post-conflict countries.

The plan was to deploy members of the corps when needed, apply the lessons they had learned in past conflicts, and make the office a center of expertise, authority, planning, and training. But Congress granted little funding to the new office, and existing State Department offices declined to yield authority to it. Throughout the Bush administration, the Civilian Response Corps remained primarily a database of names.

Hillary Clinton tried to increase the office's authority. Elevating and renaming it as part of her reorganization of the State Department, she created the Bureau of Conflict and Stabilization Operations in 2011. Its director was Rick Barton, an expert on post-conflict stabilization efforts who had created a well-respected rapid response team at USAID known as the Office of Transition Initiatives.

Barton's philosophy was to carry out short-term initiatives that focused on building up local capacity. Instead of creating new American programs, the bureau looked for promising local government initiatives that American funding could expand. Barton minimized the number of Americans involved and invested as much authority as possible in local officials, leaders, and staff. He launched pilot efforts in Kenya and Myanmar and Honduras, but the bureau's biggest project by far was working with moderate members of the Syrian opposition in Turkey.

Working with other State Department offices and USAID, Barton hoped to increase the ability of moderate members of the Syrian opposition to deliver government services in towns and cities they controlled within Syria. Alongside Britain and other European countries, they trained Syrian local government officials, journalists, and human rights activists and gave them small cash grants and equipment, such as satellite phones, generators, and fire trucks. The goal was to boost the credibility of moderate Syrians as compared to jihadists battling Assad. But members of the Syrian opposition bitterly complained that the program—which only delivered nonlethal assistance—was plagued with backlogs and delays.

Ward, the USAID official who served in Afghanistan and Libya and oversaw procurement, was sent to Turkey to coordinate the nonlethal assistance effort in 2012. He praised Barton's approach but said that the State Department and USAID, yet again, did not have the capacity to deliver aid due to personnel shortages.

Members of Congress enacted a law mandating that any Syrian who received American assistance have their name and biographical information run through multiple American databases. The idea was to ensure that no American aid went to Syrians with ties to extremist groups. Ward said he and his colleagues agreed with the measure but that they lacked the personnel to enter the biographical information into the databases.

"It's a good law; we support it," he said in a telephone interview in November 2013. "But the administrative burden of vetting that many people has a big cost. It's one State and AID have to confront if we're going to be effective in a conflict like Syria."

Conclusion

Americans, chastened by Iraq, Afghanistan, and an anemic U.S. economy, are understandably tired of the region. When it comes to the Middle East, they want as little to do with the area as possible.

But while the temptation to disengage from the Middle East is understandable, that goal is not realistic. Even as new techniques for extracting oil and natural gas make the United States energy independent, instability in the region will have an enormous impact on the world economy. For decades to come, the economies of China, India, and Europe will remain dependent on Middle Eastern oil. In a globalized world economy, a crisis in Europe or China imperils the American economy as well.

At the same time, terrorist attacks emanating from the region will remain a dire threat to political fortunes of any American president. And barring a major realignment in American politics, Israel's security will continue to be viewed as a vital American interest.

As stated in the introduction, the goal of this book is not to trumpet a simplistic new doctrine or strategy for the United States in the region.

No single approach can apply to such a dizzyingly complex area and era. But a handful of lessons did emerge during my reporting.

In southern Afghanistan, Chuck Grader and other Americans realized that the most effective development projects were small, long-term efforts that were planned, controlled, and run by local officials and communities. Afghanistan's successful health care reform, its new mobile phone system, and the National Solidarity village grant program were all examples.

In Baghdad, Paul Bremer and Bernard Kerik discovered that providing "law and order first" is the core responsibility of any ruler, whether a local dictator or a foreign occupier. And without a massive local or foreign effort, restoring security after it has eroded is virtually impossible.

Richard Holbrooke learned that forty years after Vietnam, the White House, State Department, and Congress still struggle to carry out sophisticated diplomatic and developmental initiatives overseas. He also saw that deploying hundreds of State Department officials and spending billions on a "civilian surge" had little impact without effective local partners.

In Pakistan's tribal areas, George W. Bush and Barack Obama used drones to kill al-Qaeda leaders, but the attacks failed to significantly weaken local militant groups. Drone strikes are no substitute for the difficult process of ending the Pakistani army's sheltering of jihadists, creating a functional Pakistani government, and fostering desperately needed economic growth.

State Department officials saw the hollowness of contractors' promises that they could perform any task. While Wall Street executives grew rich, contracting companies provided minimal services and paid scant attention to whether the government's strategic goals were being achieved.

Surveying the post–Arab Spring, Turkey showed how free-market reforms, consumerism, and technological change can help transform a country. It also showed why strengthening political institutions in the region is more important than bolstering individual leaders. During the 2000s, Recep Tayyip Erdogan was a moderate Islamist who enacted sweeping political and economic reforms. In 2013, the Taksim Square protesters Erdogan crushed were the reason for hope.

Tunisia's nascent tech sector, like that of Turkey, Pakistan, Egypt, and the West Bank, is a promising example of how technological change can accelerate development. The intersection of technology, entrepreneurship. and globalization remains an enormous opportunity that an archaic State Department is failing to exploit.

In post-Qaddafi Libya, as in Afghanistan and Iraq, outside powers eager for a quick fix tried to co-opt militias instead of carrying out the long, difficult process of training government security forces. Criminals, jihadists, and tribesmen grew empowered and enriched. Moderates grew weaker.

Examining the Obama administration's performance, the White House deserves credit for mounting no new American ground invasions in the Middle East. But its confused response to the Arab Spring has undermined the credibility of the United States with both allies and foes. And its minimalist approach does not meet the historic challenges that are emerging.

American military force should be employed less in the region, and Washington cannot dictate events. But the risk-taking, activist diplomacy so far displayed by Secretary of State John Kerry can and must be carried out as well. And if the United States threatens to use military force to defend its "vital interests" in the region, it must be prepared to do so as a last resort.

The White House's extraordinarily tight control of foreign policy marginalizes the State Department. Despite reforms by Hillary Clinton, the department remains antiquated, hierarchical, and deeply risk averse. Five years after Obama has taken office, the United States' civilian national security institutions remain weak. His tenure shows the need for the United States to be more humble in the Middle East but also more knowledgeable, patient and consistent.

Skepticism regarding what, if anything, the United States can achieve in the region is understandable. Geopolitical realities— from the world economy's thirst for cheap oil to American presidents' need to stop terrorist attacks to Washington's close alliance with Israel—limit radical change. Developing new approaches is difficult.

While America's influence has clearly waned, other forces are at work that the United States can take advantage of in the region. Globalization's impact is real and irreversible. From the information revolution that helped spark the Arab Spring to the Western-style consumerism transforming urban centers, the region is more integrated into the global economy and culture than it has been in decades.

Public opinion polls show that majorities in the region support many of the same global norms as Americans: accountable governments, individual rights, and economic opportunity. The overwhelming majority of Muslims I met were moderates who opposed violent extremists. Yes, they resented American heavy-handedness and what they saw as efforts to foist American cultural norms on their societies. But they also loathed armed radicals who forcibly imposed an austere form of Islam on them at gunpoint.

In its second term the Obama administration should publicly ally the United States with Arabs and South Asians who abide by democratic norms, renounce violence, and uphold individual rights, whatever their faith. A core focus of American policy should be finding ways to quietly and consistently strengthen global norms in the region.

When possible, American aid should be used to strengthen moderate political and civic groups who embrace those ideals. From governments to businesses to security forces to civil society, the more effective path is to work with local actors and have them engage their societies. They wield far more knowledge, legitimacy, and authority than any foreigner.

Identifying "moderates," of course, is enormously problematic. There is no simple definition. Groups that reject violence and embrace liberal democracy, modernity, and globalism would be a start. The Saudi royal family and their fellow Persian Gulf autocrats would not fit that definition. Nor would the Egyptian military officers who carried out the brutal crackdown on the Mulsim Brotherhood.

Rare exceptions involving imminent national security threats exist, but the United States should shift away from its decades-old view of autocrats and monarchs as sources of stability. The dynamics unleashed by the Arab uprisings are far from over. Over the long term, authoritarian rule will not withstand the internal and external pressures at work in the region.

The process will not be easy. Washington must learn to differentiate among the region's opaque organizations and movements. The Muslim Brotherhood and other Islamist political parties are far from ideal. But if they strictly abide by democratic norms, their right to participate in the electoral process should be respected. Our true enemies are jihadists bent on violently imposing their harsh interpretation of Islam by force, not religiously conservative politicians who peacefully participate in the democratic process.

American officials say they hope to create economic and political incentives that will make being part of the international system appealing to Islamists. That is the right course. Holding elected office and being responsible for creating prosperous economies, better government services, and less corruption should moderate Islamists. If they govern and fail, their popularity should erode. Crackdowns will drive them toward violence.

Some Islamic scholars are openly challenging jihadists. At great personal risk, they publicly argue that Islam and democracy are compatible. An extraordinary debate about the very nature of Islam is unfolding across the region. It is vital that American officials respect this process as it plays out.

A core problem is Washington's failure to change its outdated approach to the region. Too many American policy makers cling to an antiquated notion of national power. Military might remains vital, but trade with the United States, access to American technology, and the threat of economic and political isolation are also now potent national security tools. America's options go beyond mounting military interventions or doing nothing at all.

Across the region, trade and investment should be wielded as tools of long-term American influence. The United States should create more European Union–style economic incentives for countries that reform. Entrepreneurship programs that leverage the popularity of American technology companies should be increased. Fulbright and other educational programs should be expanded as well.

Interacting with the Islamic world economically and culturally strengthens American security; it does not threaten it. Some predominantly Muslim countries, such as Indonesia and Turkey, represent growing export markets for American companies. In 2011, a private Indonesian airline placed a $22 billion order for 230 passenger jets with Boeing, the then largest single purchase in the firm's ninety-four-year history.

As stated in the introduction, contractors are a symptom—and cause—of the decay in America's civilian foreign policy apparatus. Major budget increases for the State Department are not possible in the current fiscal climate. But improvements can be made without vast new spending.

Reforming archaic procurement, contracting, and personnel procedures will curb the issuing of enormous contracts and shift authority away from contractors. Reducing the size and cost of projects will make them easier to shield from demands for immediate results. Slowing down, working collaboratively with locals, and doing fewer things over longer periods will prove more effective.

The goal should not be to hurl tens of billions of American taxpayer dollars at the region. It should be to promote investment, education, and training that builds up local capacity. One of the gravest threats to America's security is Washington's failure to match its ambitions with its actual resources and capabilities.

Obama's Afghanistan surge showed that there are certain things the United States simply cannot achieve overseas, no matter how many troops or dollars it throws at a problem. Even if the United States perfectly executes its policies and programs, they alone will not stabilize countries. The degree of difficulty in influencing some local dynamics is simply too high. In the end, the most important actors are local. Nations must carry out reforms themselves. The United States never has been—and never will be—all-powerful.

American diplomats who have served for decades in the Middle East argue that the United States should engage across the region but be realistic about its goals. In each country, American officials should determine what issues, if any, truly impact the United States strategically.

They should make a hard-nosed determination of which of those dynamics Washington can, in fact, shape or impact without the use of military force. And they should develop realistic, carefully integrated, long-term plans for achieving their goals. If no plan seems feasible, American officials should admit that there are situations in which the United States can and should do nothing.

Most of all, the United States must avoid the trap of a perpetual war on terror. A threat exists, but we must not overreact. NSA surveillance and CIA drone strikes should continue but be limited and transparent. Local security force training and intelligence sharing should be expanded. Predominantly Muslim countries should no longer be viewed solely through the lens of counterterrorism. In the end, the most potent long-term weapons against jihadists are moderate Muslims, not American soldiers.

ACKNOWLEDGMENTS

This book would not have been possible without the brave work of scores of other journalists. As I described in the author's note at the beginning of this book, for personal reasons I have not traveled to Afghanistan, Pakistan, Egypt, or Libya since 2009. I fully acknowledge the limitations this approach placed on my reporting. The goal of this book is to spark debate, not to serve as an encyclopedic history. My apologies for any of the book's shortcomings. I take full responsibility for all mistakes, errors, and omissions.

I first want to thank the many brave people I met in South Asia and the Middle East who convinced me of this book's core thesis. Their belief in democracy, tolerance, and human rights while faced by violent attacks from jihadists deeply inspired me. They will win the historic struggle between moderates and extremists now convulsing the Islamic world.

More than any other individual, Jonathan Moore brought this book to fruition. He listened to my explanations for why I wanted to write it, counseled me on how best to do so, and then spent countless hours reading dismal drafts. His incisive comments and edits vastly improved the book. His encouragement was priceless. He is an extraordinary public servant, scholar, and friend. I am lucky to have him in my life.

My extraordinary editors at Thomson Reuters gave me an opportunity to become a columnist, allowed me to write this book, and made possible the travel it involved. This book would not have been possible without them. I thank Steven Adler, Paul Ingrassia, Chrystia Freeland, Jim Ledbetter, Paul Smalera, Allison Silver, Chadwick Matlin, and Joe Mandel. Chrystia and Jim, in particular, believed in this book and me. I am enormously grateful for all the help, encouragement, and inspiration they have given me.

Many other editors and reporters at Thomson Reuters supported this project as well and patiently waited when this book took up time, particularly Mike Williams, Stuart Karle, Alix Freedman, Jim Impoco, Kristina Cooke, and Deb Nelson.

More than any other colleague at Reuters, though, Missy Ryan, a friend and extraordinary journalist, provided insight into every aspect of this book. Her experience covering the fall of the Qaddafi regime in Libya, twenty months covering the war in Iraq, and the last two years covering American policy in Afghanistan and Pakistan have given her a unique perspective on the issues I have tried to address here. She was a constant source of encouragement and insight. My Reuters colleagues and friends Felix Salmon, Ben Walsh, Peter Rudegeair, and Uzra Khan have also been wonderful.

Editors at the *Atlantic* have been incredibly supportive and encouraging as well. For featuring my work I thank particularly David Bradley, James Bennet, Bob Cohn, John Gould, Derek Thompson, Max Fisher. Stories I wrote for Reuters and *Foreign Policy* magazine's Jim Impoco about drone warfare make up a chapter of this book. I am enormously grateful to Jim Impoco, Susan Glasser, and Blake Hounshell for their guidance, editing, and help.

A chapter I wrote about Richard Holbrooke for a 2011 book on his life, *The Unquiet American: Richard Holbrooke in the World*, serves as a chapter as well. My thanks to PublicAffairs, the publisher, as well as to my editors, Samantha Power and Derek Chollet, for their help, insight, and support.

Administrators and colleagues at Brown University were supportive as well when I taught a journalism class there while working on this book. I thank Ruth Simmons, Kevin McLaughlin, Mark Schlissel, David Kertzer, Stephen Foley, Lawrence Stanley, Elizabeth Taylor, Tracy Breton, Jonathan Readey, Marilyn Netter, Marianne Costa, Lorraine Mazza, and Ellen Viola. I thank Norman Boucher, Peter Andreas, and Michael Kennedy, and my students as well.

Many people helped with the reporting of this book. In New York, Suchi Mathur and Ruth Fecych provided invaluable research and guidance. Fred Abrahams, a senior associate with Human Rights Watch, who has been visiting Libya since 2005, provided insights into a country I have never visited. So did Youssef Gaigi, a Tunisian journalist who covered the Libyan uprising for Al Jazeera and his own new company, Tunisia Live.

In Egypt, Lauren E. Bohn conducted reporting for me on the ground and offered her valuable insights and advice. A Fulbright fellow, Overseas Press Club fellow, Pulitzer Center grantee, and assistant editor of the *Cairo Review*, Lauren was extraordinarily helpful, resourceful, and patient. Along with original reporting she did for me, I have quoted extensively from pieces she wrote for the Daily Beast, CNN, and other media. Dalia Mogahed's insights on Egypt and the region as a whole in the post–Arab Spring were enormously helpful as well.

The reporting of Elmira Bayrasli, an old friend from Bosnia, exposed me to the challenges entrepreneurs face in developing countries. She generously agreed that I could quote extensively from an excellent piece she wrote in the summer 2012 issue of the *World Policy Journal* that described two of the people in this book. Her forthcoming book *Steve Jobs Lives in Pakistan: Extraordinary Entrepreneurs in the Developing World* will be an even greater contribution to the topic.

In Tunisia, Youssef Gaigi, Zied Mhirsi, Farah Samti, and many others from Tunisia Live were incredibly helpful before, during, and after my reporting trip there.

In Turkey, Nevra Yarac and Selcuk Tepeli were incredible reporters, guides, and friends. In a second trip to Turkey, Syrian refugee Mahmoud Mosa helped me report in refugee camps and understand the tragedy unfolding in his country. The work of Erika Solomon and other Reuters colleagues who bravely reported in Syrian was invaluable.

In Afghanistan and Pakistan, the friendships and reporting of Carlotta Gall, Tim Golden, and Declan Walsh helped me tremendously, as did the work of many Afghan and Pakistani journalists whose names I will not mention for safety reasons. The Iraq chapter of this book is based entirely on reporting I did with my friend and colleague Michael Moss at the *New York Times*. He is an extraordinary journalist, person, and friend.

Along with teaching me journalism, the *Times* saved the lives of two Afghan journalists, Tahir Luddin and Asad Mangal, and me when we were kidnapped by the Taliban in November 2008. I will always regret what Tahir, Asad, and their families went through. I apologize to them and their families, and thank all of them for their tremendous understanding and bravery.

The *Times*'s tireless efforts over seven months to win our release convinced our captors that we were worth keeping alive. That gave us the opportunity to wait for a chance to escape. I thank Pakistan Army Major Nadeem Khattack for allowing us onto his military base in the middle of the night after Tahir and I escaped as our guard slept. Thanks to the efforts of the *Times* and Asad's family, Asad returned home safely six weeks later.

I will always be enormously grateful to Arthur Sulzberger Jr., Bill Keller, Jill Abramson, Dean Baquet, Susan Chira, John Geddes, William Schmidt, David McCraw, Matt Purdy, Christine Kay, and so many other longtime friends at the *Times* for their help in New York. They saved our lives.

In Afghanistan, Carlotta Gall, Chris Chivers, Adam Ellick, Rich Oppel, and my amazing Afghan colleagues and friends worked tirelessly to help us. In Pakistan, Ismail Khan, Salman Masood, Beena Sarwar, Pir Zubair Shah, Jane Perlez, and many others did as well. Their work on our behalf endangered them, and I will always be grateful for what they did.

Many other friends, experts, and officials helped enormously and devoted tremendous amounts of time, energy, and resources to our case, particularly Michael Semple, Richard Holbrooke, Kati Marton, Samantha Power, Karl and Ching Eikenberry, Marin Strmecki, Kay McGowan, Tim Golden, Michael Moss, and Peter Bergen.

Mark Mazzetti, Eric Schmitt, Douglas Franz, Ahmed Rashid, and Barbara Quinn provided generous expertise as well. I admire, respect, and salute the courage, sacrifice, and bravery of Sultan Munadi, Daniel Pearl, Piotr Stanczak, Bowe Bergdahl, and all journalists who remain in captivity.

I will always be enormously grateful to my editors and friends at the *Christian Science Monitor* who helped me when the Bosnian Serbs detained me for ten days in 1995. David Cook, Clayton Jones, Faye Bowers, and many others have my eternal gratitude.

The reporting, help, and friendship of many colleagues at the *New York Times* made this book possible and inspired and encouraged me for years. They include Anthony Shadid, Joe Kahn, David D. Kirkpatrick, Neil MacFarquhar, Anne Barnard, Tim Arango, David E. Sanger, Tyler Hicks, Dexter Filkins, Marcus Mabry, Roger Cohen, Graham Bowley, Rob Mackey, Scott Shane, Thom Shanker, Alissa

Rubin, Graham Bowley, Rod Nordland, Robert Worth, and many others. Earlier in my career, Chris Isham, Richard Greenberg, and Aram Roston gave me a chance and inspired me at ABC News. Paul Jablow and Linda Linley did the same at the *Philadelphia Inquirer.*

This book is filled with work of other journalists from across the Middle East and South Asia, including Rajiv Chandrasekaran, Ahmed Rashid, Josh Paltrow, Ken Dilanian, Adam Entous, Siobhan Gorman, Julian Barnes, Peter Finn, Greg Miller, Karen DeYoung, David Finkel, Dana Priest, Bob Woodward, James Dobbins, Seth Jones, Louisa Loveluck, Laura Rozen, Thomas Mann, William Dobson, Tarek Osman, Pratap Chatterjee, Milan Vaishnav, and Daniel Cutherell. Many current and former government officials in Washington and across the region helped me but wish to remain anonymous. I thank them as well.

Many friends helped me over the years while working on this book. Eric and Sylvan Wold, Julian Borger, Paul Salopek, Greg Scholl, Chloe Breyer, Marcello Picone, Ivan Obregon, Salman Ahmed, Elliot Thomson, Julian Borger, Kathleen Reen, Ivan Obregon, Lisa Ferrari, Kannan Sundaram, Don Nay, the Bissell family, Paul Haven, Victoria Burnett, Barry Bearak, Gary Bass, and George Packer have my thanks.

Emma Daly, Santiago Lyon, Stacy Sullivan, Laura Pitter, Jonathan Landay, Katie Moore, Kit Roane, Katya Jestin, Joel Brand, Ben Ward, Leigh Cheng, John Bastian, Pete Brandt, Al Erickson, Matt Borger, Rod Peterson, Damon Struyk, Jim Williamson, Bob Perkins, Steve Cote, Jim Webb, Jay, Joe and Doris Brenchick, and Rocky and Martha Manoriti do as well. Vincent Manoriti, Denise Morgan, Mary Anne Schwalbe, Sultan Munadi, and Peter Boisvert will always inspire me.

Last and most important, I thank the people who created this book. Sarah Chalfant has been a tireless friend, editor, and agent for more than fifteen years. I thank her for all she has done to make this book a reality. Editors at Viking took a risk on a book at a time when Americans have grown enormously tired of the region. I thank Clare Ferraro, Linda Cowen, Barbara Campo, Margaret Riggs, Randee Marullo, Jane Cavolina, and Josh Karpf, who patiently put up with rapidly changing events in the region and missed deadlines. Carolyn Coleburn, Bennett Petrone, and Meredith Burks did extraordinary work promoting the book as well.

My editor at Viking, Wendy Wolf, is more responsible for this book's existence than anyone else. She took research I had conducted for an initial book on Afghanistan and had the vision to turn it into something much more forward-looking. Our kidnapping seemed to end my dream of writing a book about the post-9/11 decade. Wendy resurrected that dream. I will always be enormously grateful to her. I could not have had a more patient, supportive, and insightful editor. I thank her for believing in this book.

Finally, I thank my family. My parents, Carol and Harvey; siblings Lee, Laura, and Erik; stepparents Andrea and George; and stepbrothers, Daniel and Joel; and many aunts, uncles, nieces, nephews, and cousins. They have showered me with love and have endured years of worry, and they all dropped everything and performed heroically— particularly Lee—when I needed them most. My in-laws—Jim and Mary Jane, Christie, Chris, Karen, Jason, Howard, and Christina— have put up with the same stresses for fewer years and given enormous support, love, and encouragement for a new family member.

My wife, Kristen, has endured more in four years of marriage than many spouses experience in a lifetime. She recognized the importance of this book and supported me throughout the reporting and writing of it. I thank her for her encouragement, patience, and love. Today I am living the life of my dreams. It is all because of her.

NOTES

INTRODUCTION

Page

xiii **and the spending of more than $1 trillion:** For a detailed accounting of spending since the 9/11 attacks, see Amy Belasco, *The Cost of Iraq, Afghanistan, and Other Global War on Terror Operations Since 9/11*, Congressional Research Service, March 29, 2011, http://www.fas.org/sgp/crs/natsec/RL33110.pdf.

 xv **At the peak:** See Commission on Wartime Contracting, *Transforming Wartime Contracting: Controlling Costs, Reducing Risks: Final Report to Congress*, August 2011, 30–31, http://www.wartimecontracting.gov/docs/CWC_FinalReport-lowres.pdf.

 xv **was sometimes more costly:** Ibid., 39–40.

 xv **waste, fraud, and abuse:** Ibid., 2, 5.

 xvi **95 percent:** See Belasco.

 xvi **in political life:** See Pew Research Center, *Most Muslims Want Democracy, Personal Freedoms, and Islam in Public Life*, July 10, 2012, http://www.pewglobal.org/2012/07/10/most muslims-want-democracy-personal-freedoms-and-islam-in-political-life/.

 xvi **ways of doing business:** See Pew Research Center, *Global Opinion of Obama Slips, International Policies Faulted*, June 13, 2012, http://www

.pewglobal.org/2012/06/13/chapter-2-attitudes-toward-american
-culture-and-ideas/.

xvi **tens of millions of jobs will need to be created in the region by 2020:** See
Sara Hamdan, "Jobs and Age Reign in Risk Factors for Mideast Uprisings,"
New York Times, February 2, 2011, http://www.nytimes.com/2011/02/03
/world/middleeast/03iht-m03job.html?pagewanted=all.

CHAPTER 1: LITTLE AMERICA

3 **wean Afghans from Soviet influence:** See Cynthia Clapp-Wincek, *The
Helmand Valley Project in Afghanistan,* USAID, December 1983, 1–3. The
full report is a detailed history and assessment of the Helmand project.

3 **"Little America":** For elegant descriptions of cold war Lashkar Gah,
see Arnold Toynbee, *Between Oxus and Jumna* (1961), and Nancy
Hatch Dupree, *An Historical Guide to Afghanistan* (1977). For an exhaustive collection of the USAID-commissioned studies of the projects
during the cold war, see Richard Scott, "Scott's Helmand Valley Ar-
chives," at www.scottshelmandvalleyarchives.org.

4 **loftier, long-term goals:** Louis Dupree is very critical of the project, par-
ticularly in its early phases; see Louis Dupree, *Afghanistan* (1970), 482–
85, 497, 499–507, 634–35. Nick Cullather also criticizes the project; see
Nick Cullather, "Damming Afghanistan: Modernization in a Buffer
State," *Journal of American History* 89, no. 2 (September 2002): 512–37.
For USAID descriptions of the project, see Lloyd Baron, *Sector Analysis:
Helmand-Arghandab Valley Region,* USAID, February 1973, 2, 7–9; and
Mildred Caudill, *Helmand-Arghandab Valley: Yesterday, Today, Tomorrow,* USAID, 1969, 31. Residents of Helmand and former USAID officials
generally praised the project in interviews conducted in Afghanistan
between 2004 and 2008 and in the United States between 2004 and 2012.

5 **Karakul fur:** See Cullather, 512–17.

8 **"We felt that we were free now":** See David Rohde, "An Afghan Symbol
for Change, Then Failure," *New York Times,* September 5, 2006, http://
www.nytimes.com/2006/09/05/world/asia/05afghan.html.

10 **$130,000 a year:** Interviews with Grader and USAID officials in Af-
ghanistan.

19 **Rory Donohoe:** See David Rohde, "Taliban Raise Poppy Production to

a Record Again," *New York Times,* August 26, 2007, http://www.nytimes.com/2007/08/26/world/asia/26heroin.html?pagewanted=all.

25 **In 2010, a series of studies:** See *Afghanistan Mortality Survey: 2010 Health Study Shows Significant Gains in Afghan Maternal and Child Health,* USAID, January 30, 2012, http://transition.usaid.gov/locations/afghanistanpakistan/countries/afghanistan/ams2010.html.

26 **National Solidarity Program:** See *Afghanistan's National Solidarity Program Has Reached Thousands of Afghan Communities, but Faces Challenges That Could Limit Outcomes,* Office of the Special Inspector General for Afghanistan Reconstruction, March 22, 2011, www.sigar.mil/pdf/audits/2011-03-22audit-11-08.pdf.

26 **Ministry of Communications and Information Technology:** See Javid Hamdard, *The State of Telecommunications and Internet in Afghanistan: Six Years Later (2006–2012),* Internews, April 19, 2012, http://www.internews.org/research-publications/state-telecommunications-and-internet-afghanistan-six-years-later-2006-2012.

27 **spent nearly $1.3 billion:** See Rajiv Chandrasekaran, "Cost of War in Afghanistan Will Be Major Factor in Troop-Reduction Talks," *Washington Post,* May 30, 2011, http://www.washingtonpost.com/world/national-security/cost-of-war-in-afghanistan-will-be-major-factor-in-troop-reduction-talks/2011/05/27/AGR8z2EH_print.html.

30 **shot dead an Afghan colleague:** See Abdul Malek, "South African Contractor Held for Killing Afghan Guard," Reuters, October 3, 2009, http://www.reuters.com/article/2009/10/03/us-afghanistan-contractor-sb-idUSTRE5921HJ20091003.

30 **The *Washington Post* reported:** See Rajiv Chandrasekaran, "U.S. Pursues a New Way to Rebuild in Afghanistan," *Washington Post,* June 19, 2009, http://www.washingtonpost.com/wp-dyn/content/article/2009/06/18/AR2009061804135.html.

30 **systematic overbilling:** See Marisa Taylor and Warren P. Strobel, "U.S. Contractor Accused of Fraud Still Winning Big Afghan Projects," McClatchy, September 19, 2010, http://www.mcclatchydc.com/2010/09/19/100690/us-contractor-accused-of-fraud.html.

30 **pleaded guilty:** See "Husband and Wife Co-owners of Subcontracting Company Plead Guilty to Contract Fraud Related to Afghanistan Re-

building," Office of Public Affairs, Department of Justice, September 9, 2009, http://www.justice.gov/opa/pr/2009/September/09=crm=943 .html.

CHAPTER 2: LAW AND DISORDER IN IRAQ

32 **Jay Garner:** See Michael Moss and David Rohde, "Law and Disorder: Misjudgments Marred U.S. Plans for Iraqi Police," *New York Times,* May 21, 2006, http://www.nytimes.com/2006/05/21/world/middleeast/21 security.html?pagewanted=all; and Michael Moss, "Law and Disorder: How Iraq Police Reform Became a Casualty of War," *New York Times,* May 22, 2006, http://www.nytimes.com/2006/05/22/world/middleeast /22security.html?pagewanted=all.

35 **would be left to the Iraqi police:** Ibid.

35 **U.S. Army Lieutenant Colonel Robert Waltemeyer:** See David Rohde, "Deadly Unrest Leaves a Town Bitter at U.S.," *New York Times,* April 20, 2003, http://www.nytimes.com/2003/04/20/world/a-nation -at-war-mosul-deadly-unrest-leaves-a-town-bitter-at-us.html.

36 **Rumsfeld said:** See Moss and Rohde.

37 **he recalled:** Ibid.

43 **"The police are working":** Ibid.

43 **released from prison in May 2013:** See Clem Richardson, "Bernie Kerik Copes with Prison Life," *New York Daily News,* June 13, 2012, http://articles.nydailynews.com/2012-06-13/news/32199756_1_bernie -kerik-hala-matli-bernard-kerik.

43 **in the next thirty days:** See Moss and Rohde (2006) and Moss (2006).

46 **"Some were just sitting":** Ibid.

46 **"qualified personnel":** Ibid.

48 **$1 billion:** See Business Wire, "DynCorp International Inc. to Be Acquired by Cerberus Capital Management, L.P.," April 12, 2010, http:// www.businesswire.com/news/home/20100412006033/en/DynCorp -International-Acquired-Cerberus-Capital-Management-L.P.

49 **sale of DynCorp:** Ibid.; and see Greg Roumeliotis, "McKeon, Founder of PE Firm Veritas, Committed Suicide," Reuters, September 14, 2012; http://www.reuters.com/article/2012/09/14/us-veritas-death-idUSBRE 88D1CS20120914.

CHAPTER 3: A CIVILIAN SURGE

50 **shuttering Guantánamo:** See Peter Finn, "Obama's Plan to Shutter Guantanamo Faces Hurdles," *Washington Post,* January 22, 2009, http://www.washingtonpost.com/wp-dyn/content/article/2009/01/21/AR2009012101036.html.

50 **a robust civilian surge:** See David Rohde, "The Last Mission," in *The Unquiet American: Richard Holbrooke in the World,* ed. Derek Chollet and Samantha Power (2011), 282–83.

51 **and spanned five presidencies:** Ibid.; and see James Mann, *The Obamians* (2012), 229–40.

53 **he hired him as well:** See George Packer, "The Last Mission: Richard Holbrooke's Plan to Avoid the Mistakes of Vietnam in Afghanistan," *New Yorker,* September 28, 2009, http://m.newyorker.com/reporting/2009/09/28/090928fa_fact_packer?currentPage=all.

56 **AED, meanwhile, rode the:** See Dana Hedgpeth and Josh Boak, "USAID Suspends District-Based Nonprofit AED from Contracts amid Investigation," *Washington Post,* December 8, 2010, http://www.washingtonpost.com/wp-dyn/content/article/2010/12/08/AR2010120807665.html.

56 **pay back the government:** See "Washington, D.C.–Based Academy for Educational Development Pays More Than $5 Million to Settle False Claims Act Allegations," Office of Public Affairs, Department of Justice, June 30, 2011, http://www.justice.gov/usao/dc/news/2011/jun/11-278.pdf.

56 **was paid $879,530:** See Ken Dilanian, "Review: High Salaries for Aid Group CEOs," *USA Today,* September 1, 2009, http://www.usatoday.com/news/world/2009-08-31-us-aid-groups_N.htm#chart.

57 **"This dinner is over":** See Rajiv Chandrasekaran, *Little America* (2012), 89.

58 **could be cathartic:** Based on interviews with several former aides to Holbrooke and administration officials who agreed to speak with me only on condition that their names not be made public.

60 **would speak to Karzai:** Ibid.

60 **were plotting against him:** Ibid.

63 **"vital national security interests":** See Laurence Arnold, "Richard Holbrooke, U.S. Diplomat from Vietnam to Afghanistan, Dies Aged 69,"

Bloomberg, December 14, 2010, http://www.bloomberg.com/news/2010
-12-14/richard-holbrooke-u-s-diplomat-from-vietnam-to-afghanistan
-dies-aged-69.html.

64 **"opposition from others"**: See Chollet and Power, 287.

66 **became a sign of progress**: See Chandrasekaran, 197–99.

66 **"If that money could have been spread out"**: Interviews and e-mail
exchanges with Dempsey in 2011 and 2012.

67 **Holbrooke's insatiable ego**: Interviews with former administration officials and Holbrooke's aides.

67 **when Holbrooke was out of town**: See Chandrasekaran, 197–99.

67 **meeting between Karzai and Obama**: Ibid.

68 **that Holbrooke be included**: Ibid.

CHAPTER 4: THE RISE OF THE DRONE

69 **felt toward the United States**: See Chollet and Power, 291–93.

71 **calling the conditions "humiliating"**: See Omar Waraich, "How a U.S.
Aid Package Could Threaten Zardari," *Time,* October 8, 2009, http://
www.time.com/time/world/article/0,8599,1929306,00.html.

72 **"reasonable period for the latter"**: See Laura Rozen, "Dissent Memo:
USAID Official Charges Holbrooke Pakistan Aid Plan Flawed," *Politico,*
October 12, 2009, http://www.politico.com/blogs/laurarozen/1009
/Dissent_Memo_USAID_official_charges_Holbrooke_Pakistan_aid
_plan_flawed.html.

73 **respond to their requests quickly**: See Chollet and Power, 291–93.

75 **military ID cards, and a camera**: See Declan Walsh, "A CIA Spy, a Hail of
Bullets, Three Killed and a US-Pakistan Diplomatic Row," *Guardian,* February 20, 2011, http://www.guardian.co.uk/world/2011/feb/20/cia-agent
-lahore-civilian-deaths; and Asif Chaudhry, "US Official Guns Down Two
Motorcyclists in Lahore," *Dawn,* January 28, 2011, http://dawn.com
/2011/01/28/us-official-guns-down-two-motorcyclists-in-lahore/.

76 **Pakistani officials flatly disagreed**: See Greg Miller and Karen De-
Young, "U.S., Pakistani Officials at Diplomatic Odds in Fatal Shooting,"
Washington Post, February 10, 2011, http://www.washingtonpost.com
/wp-dyn/content/article/2011/02/09/AR2011020906436.html.

76 **working as a contractor for the CIA**: See Declan Walsh and Ewan Mac-

Askill, "American Who Sparked Diplomatic Crisis over Lahore Shooting Was CIA Spy," *Guardian,* February 20, 2011, http://www.guardian.co.uk/ world/2011/feb/20/us-raymond-davis-lahore-cia; and Mark Mazzetti, Ashley Parker, Jane Perlez, and Eric Schmitt, "American Held in Pakistan Worked with CIA," *New York Times,* February 21, 2011, http://www.ny times.com/2011/02/22/world/asia/22pakistan.html?pagewanted=all.

76 **American intelligence agencies were contractors:** See Dana Priest and William M. Arkin, "A Hidden World, Growing Beyond Control," *Washington Post,* July 19, 2010, http://projects.washingtonpost.com/top -secret-america/articles/a-hidden-world-growing-beyond-control/.

77 **scale up the size of the organization:** Ibid.

77 **rapidly increase its workforce:** Ibid.

77 **eight years in prison:** See Agence France-Presse, "Court Upholds CIA Contractor's Detainee Abuse Conviction," August 11, 2009, http://www .google.com/hostednews/afp/article/ALeqM5gSo6iRtgbNNlDhDyO _VcZEmT45MQ.

78 **"fuel our cars and run our factories":** See Macon Phillips, "President Barack Obama's Inaugural Address," The White House, January 21, 2009, http://www.whitehouse.gov/blog/inaugural-address.

78 **created instability, not stability:** See David Rohde, "The Obama Doctrine: How the President's Drone War Is Backfiring," *Foreign Policy,* March/April 2012, http://www.foreignpolicy.com/articles/2012/02/27 /the_obama_doctrine?page=full.

80 **thirty-three drone strikes in total:** Ibid.

80 **The CIA quickly killed the plan:** Ibid.; interviews with former administration officials; and see Dennis C. Blair, "Drones Alone Are Not the Answer," *New York Times,* August 14, 2012, http://www.nytimes.com /2011/08/15/opinion/drones-alone-are-not-the-answer.html.

80 **ignored Munter's protests:** See Adam Entous, Siobhan Gorman, and Julian E. Barnes, "U.S. Tightens Drone Rules," *Wall Street Journal,* November 4, 2011, http://online.wsj.com/article/SB100014240529702046 21 904577013982672973836.html.

81 **Davis was released on March 16:** See *BBC,* "Pakistan Anger over Release of CIA Killer Raymond Davis," March 17, 2011, www.bbc.co.uk /news/world-south-asia-12769714.

81 **over a bagel shop parking spot:** See Lee Ferran, "Raymond Davis, CIA Contractor, Charged with Felony in Parking Lot Skirmish," ABC News, October 4, 2011, http://abcnews.go.com/Blotter/raymond-davis-cia -contractor-charged-parking-lot-fight/story?id=14663216.

81 **an unusual public statement:** See Sebastian Abbot, "Pakistan Army Chief Condemns US Drone Attack," Associated Press, March 17, 2011, http://o.seattletimes.nwsource.com/html/nationworld/2014522314 _apaspakistan.html.

81 **"not a charity car wash":** Ibid.

82 **more than twenty people:** Interviews with former administration officials; and see *Dawn*, "Rare Condemnation by PM, Army Chief: 40 Killed in Drone Attack," March 18, 2011, http://dawn.com/2011/03/18/rare -condemnation-by-pm-army-chief-40-killed-in-drone-attack/; and Entous, Gorman, and Barnes.

82 **over the signature strikes:** See Entous, Gorman, and Barnes.

83 **during the same period in 2010:** See Counterterrorism Strategy Initiative, *The Year of the Drone: An Analysis of U.S. Drone Strikes in Pakistan, 2004–2012*, New American Foundation, August 24, 2012, http://counter terrorism.newamerica.net/drones.

83 **to review the attacks:** See Dianne Feinstein, "Letters: Sen. Feinstein on Drone Attacks," *Los Angeles Times*, May 17, 2012, http://articles.latimes .com/2012/may/17/opinion/la-le-0517-thursday-feinstein-drones -20120517.

83 **a 14-percentage-point rise from 2008:** See Pew Global Attitudes Project, *Pakistani Public Opinion Ever More Critical of U.S.* (Overview), Pew Research Center, June 27, 2012, http://www.pewglobal.org/2012/06/27 /pakistani-public-opinion-ever-more-critical-of-u-s/; and Pew Global Attitudes Project, *Pakistani Public Opinion Ever More Critical of U.S.* (Chapter 1: Views of the U.S. And American Foreign Policy), Pew Research Center, June 27, 2012, http://www.pewglobal.org/2012/06/27 /chapter-1-views-of-the-u-s-and-american-foreign-policy-5/.

87 **the challenges entrepreneurs face:** See Elmira Bayrasli, "Entrepreneurs Save the World," *World Policy Journal*, Summer 2012, http://www .worldpolicy.org/journal/summer2012/entrepreneurs-save-the-world.

CHAPTER 5: WHERE ISLAM AND DEMOCRACY MEET, UNEASILY

93 **the country's disenfranchised Shiite majority:** "Arab Spring, Fall, and After," *New York Times,* February 21, 2012, http://www.nytimes.com/interactive/2011/11/23/world/middleeast/Arab-Spring-and-Fall.html.

94 *Milliyet* **wrote:** See Tim Arango and Hwaida Saad, "Turkey's Parliament Backs Military Measures on Syria," *New York Times,* October 4, 2012, http://www.nytimes.com/2012/10/05/world/middleeast/syria.html?pagewanted=all.

94 **40-million-strong middle class:** See World Factbook, *Country Comparison: GDP—Real Growth Rate 2012,* Central Intelligence Agency (accessed August 29, 2012), https://www.cia.gov/library/publications/the-world-factbook/rankorder/2003rank.html?countryName=Turkey&countryCode=tu&regionCode=mde&rank=15#tu.

94 **to silence dissent:** See Dexter Filkins, "The Deep State," *New Yorker,* March 12, 2012, http://www.newyorker.com/reporting/2012/03/12/120312fa_fact_filkins.

95 **political reform:** See David Rohde, "Where Islam and Democracy Meet, Uneasily," Reuters, October 21, 2011, http://www.reuters.com/article/2011/10/21/idUS209035153320111021.

95 **soap operas:** See David Rohde, "The Islamic World's Culture War, Played Out on TV Soap Operas," *Atlantic,* March 9, 2012, http://www.theatlantic.com/international/archive/2012/03/the-islamic-worlds-culture-war-played-out-on-tv-soap-operas/254247/.

96 **"a negative light":** See Ece Toksabay and Ibon Villelabeitia, "Sultan's TV Drama Opens Turkish Divide on Religion," Reuters, February 8, 2011, http://www.reuters.com/article/2011/02/08/us-turkey-ottoman-drama-idUSTRE7173GA20110208.

96 **toned down:** See Rohde, "The Islamic World's Culture War, Played Out on TV Soap Operas."

96 **a phenomenal hit:** See Robert F. Worth, "Arab TV Tests Societies' Limits with Depictions of Sex and Equality," *New York Times,* September 26, 2008, http://www.nytimes.com/2008/09/27/world/middleeast/27beirut.html.

97 **85 million viewers:** See AMEinfo.com, "Beirut Hosts the 2nd New Arab Woman Forum (NAWF)," September 11, 2008, http://www.ameinfo.com/168434.html.

97 **and groundbreaking:** See Worth.

97 **divorces occurred in several countries:** See Al Arabiya News, "Turkish Soap Star Sparks Divorces in Arab World," June 29, 2008, http://www.alarabiya.net/articles/2008/06/29/52291.html.

97 **Islamic clerics denounced *Noor*:** See Andy Sambidge, "MBC Expands Soap Opera Shows Despite Mufti Fury," *Arabian Business,* October 21, 2008, http://www.arabianbusiness.com/mbc-expands-soap-opera-shows-despite-mufti-fury-84564.html; and Worth.

98 **received glowing coverage:** See Nadia Bilbassy-Charters, "Leave It to Turkish Soap Operas to Conquer Hearts and Minds," *Foreign Policy,* April 15, 2010, http://mideast.foreignpolicy.com/posts/2010/04/15/leave_it_to_turkish_soap_operas_to_conquer_hearts_and_minds; and Owen Matthews, "The Arab World's 'Dallas,'" *Newsweek*, September 5, 2011, http://www.thedailybeast.com/newsweek/2011/09/04/turkish-soap-operas-are-sweeping-the-middle-east.html.

98 **the Coen brothers of Turkey:** See Rohde, "The Islamic World's Culture War, Played Out on TV Soap Operas."

98 **victory tour of the region:** See Rohde, "Where Islam and Democracy Meet, Uneasily."

99 **"can run a state very successfully":** See Cecile Feuillatre, "Buoyant Erdogan Sells Turkish Model to Arab Spring," Agence France-Presse, September 14, 2012, http://www.google.com/hostednews/afp/article/ALeqM5iYbCJEmBCnS-3bEXWY9mkdKHxSwA.

100 **drafted after a 1980 military coup:** See Rohde, "Where Islam and Democracy Meet, Uneasily."

101 **in emerging market countries:** See Bayrasli.

101 **wireless routers designed for American drywall:** Ibid.

105 **transform a country:** See Bartlomiej Kaminski and Francis Ng, *Turkey's Evolving Trade Integration into Pan-European Markets: World Bank Policy Research Working Paper 3908,* World Bank, May 2006.

CHAPTER 6: THE SILICON VALLEY OF THE ARAB WORLD?

106 **"Muslim communities around the world":** See "Remarks by the President on a New Beginning," Office of the Press Secretary, The White House, June 4, 2009, http://www.whitehouse.gov/the-press-office /remarks-president-cairo-university-6-04-09.

107 **officials thought the uprisings:** See David E. Sanger, *Confront and Conceal: Obama's Secret Wars and Surprising Use of American Power* (2012), 283–88.

107 **for training and mentoring:** See David Rohde, "Can Tunisia Become the Silicon Valley of the Arab World?," *Atlantic*, March 30, 2012, http://www.whitehouse.gov/the-press-office/remarks-president-cairo-university-6-04-09.

109 **A 2012 survey found that:** See Pew Global Attitudes Project, *Most Muslims Want Democracy, Personal Freedoms, and Islam in Political Life*.

109 **growth it enjoyed between 1997 and 2007:** See Daniel Loehr, "IMF Recommends a Control on Public Expenditures," *Tunisia Live*, August 6, 2012, http://www.tunisia-live.net/2012/08/06/imf-recommends-a-control-on-public-expenditures/.

111 **that unnerved Tunisian moderates:** See Ahmed Ellali, "Several Thousand Salafists Demonstrate for Islamic Law, Attack Dramatists in Tunis," *Tunisia Live*, March 25, 2012, http://www.tunisia-live.net /2012/03/25/several-thousand-salafists-demonstrate-for-islamic-law-attack-dramatists-in-tunis/; and Tarek Amara and Lin Noueihed, "Tunisian Salafi Islamists Riot over 'Insulting' Art," Reuters, June 12, 2012, http://www.reuters.com/article/2012/06/12/us-tunisia-salafis-clash -idUSBRE85B0XW20120612; and Pesha Magid, "Union of Journalists Condemns Proposed Limits on Freedom of Press," *Tunisia Live*, August 8, 2012, http://www.tunisia-live.net/2012/08/08/union-of-journalists -condemns-proposed-limits-on-freedom-of-the-press/; and Paul Schemm, "Tunisian Democracy Threatened by Weak Opposition," Associated Press, July 4, 2012, http://bigstory.ap.org/article/tunisian-democracy-threatened-weak-opposition.

111 **in the style of Afghan Taliban:** See Bouazza Ben Bouazza and Paul Schemm, "Tunisian Radicals Travel to Syria," Associated Press,

June 21, 2012, http://bigstory.ap.org/article/tunisian-radicals-travel-syria.

CHAPTER 7: MURDER IN BENGHAZI

123 **wrote stories about him:** See David Corn and Siddhartha Mahanta, "From Libya with Love," *Mother Jones,* March 3, 2011, http://www.motherjones.com/politics/2011/03/libya-qaddafi-monitor-group; and Ed Pilkington, "The Monitor Group: Gaddafi's PR Firm Used Academics," *Guardian,* March 4, 2011, http://www.guardian.co.uk/world/2011/mar/04/the-monitor-group-gadaffi-pr.

123 **Qaddafi's son's, Saif:** See Chris Cook, "Davis Blamed over Gaddafi's Gift to LSE," *Financial Times,* December 1, 2011, http://www.ft.com/intl/cms/s/0/4971e882-1b63-11e1-85f8-00144feabdc0.html#axzz25OYSEoCM.

123 **Obama can stay forever:** See Mark Sappenfield and Tracey Samuelson, "Qaddafi UN Speech: Six Highlights—or Lowlights?" *Christian Science Monitor,* September 23, 2009, http://www.csmonitor.com/USA/Politics/The-Vote/2009/0923/qaddafi-un-speech-six-highlights-or-lowlights.

125 **blocked detainees from seeing judges:** See Fred Abrahams, "Libya Slogs Toward Democracy," *Daily Beast,* July 24, 2012, http://www.thedailybeast.com/articles/2012/07/24/with-gaddafi-gone-libya-slogs-toward-democracy.html.

126 **three thousand candidates:** Ibid.

127 **told the *New York Times*:** See Eric Schmitt, David D. Kirkpatrick, and Suliman Ali Zway, "U.S. May Have Put Mistaken Faith in Libya Site's Security," *New York Times,* October 1, 2012, http://www.nytimes.com/2012/10/01/world/africa/mistaken-sense-of-security-cited-before-envoy-to-libya-died.html?pagewanted=all.

127 **Islamic militants:** Ibid.

127 **armed Libyan fighters:** Ibid.

128 **American-made anti-Muslim video:** David Rohde, "Honoring a Slain Ambassador," Reuters, September 13, 2012, http://blogs.reuters.com/david-rohde/2012/09/13/honoring-a-slain-ambassador/.

CHAPTER 8: POST-MUBARAK

131 **Since the 1978 signing of the Camp David Accords:** See Jeremy M. Sharp, *Egypt: Transition Under Military Rule*, Congressional Research Service, June 21, 2012, 14–24, http://fpc.state.gov/documents/organiza tion/194799.pdf.

133 **dispatched Frank Wisner:** See Mark Landler, "U.S. Official with Egypt Ties to Meet with Mubarak," *New York Times*, January 31, 2011, http://www.nytimes.com/2011/02/01/world/middleeast/01diplo.html?_r=0.

133 **February 1, Mubarak made a ten-minute speech:** See "Hosni Mubarak's Speech: Full Text," *Guardian*, February 1, 2011, http://www.theguardian .com/world/2011/feb/02/president-hosni-mubarak-egypt-speech.

133 **A frustrated Obama called the Egyptian leader:** See Helene Cooper, Mark Landler, and David E. Sanger, "In U.S. Signals to Egypt, Obama Straddled a Rift," *New York Times*, February 12, 2011, http://www.nytimes .com/2011/02/13/world/middleeast/13diplomacy.html?pagewanted=all.

134 **He needs to listen:** See Office of the Press Secretary, "Remarks by President Obama and Prime Minister Stephen Harper of Canada in Joint Press Availability," The White House, February 4, 2011, http://www .whitehouse.gov/the-press-office/2011/02/04/remarks-president -obama-and-prime-minister-stephen-harper-canada-joint-p.

135 **soldiers from Saudi Arabia:** See Ethan Bronner and Michael Slackman, "Saudi Troops Enter Bahrain to Help Put Down Unrest," *New York Times*, March 14, 2011, http://www.nytimes.com/2011/03/15/world /middleeast/15bahrain.html?pagewanted=all.

135 **King Hamad declared martial law:** See David S. Cloud and Neela Banerjee, "Forces in Bahrain Move Against Crowd in Square," *Los Angeles Times*, March 16, 2011, http://articles.latimes.com/2011/mar/16/world /la-fg-bahrain-flashpoint-20110316.

135 **Carney was careful not to directly criticize:** See David E. Sanger and Eric Schmitt, "U.S.-Saudi Tensions Intensify with Mideast Turmoil," *New York Times*, March 14, 2011, http://www.nytimes.com/2011/03/15 /world/middleeast/15saudi.html?pagewanted=all.

135 **there was deep division over how to respond:** See Cooper, Landler, and Sanger.

135 **Bahrain had served as a counterweight:** See Geoff Ziezulewicz, "With Bahrain Home to 5th Fleet, U.S. Faces Dilemma over Crackdown on Protests," *Stars and Stripes*, February 12, 2012, http://www.stripes .com/with-bahrain-home-to-5th-fleet-us-faces-dilemma-over-crackdown -on-protests-1.168370.

136 **WikiLeaks cables described by the *New York Times*:** See Laura Kasinof and David E. Sanger, "U.S. Shifts to Seek Removal of Yemen's Leader, an Ally," *New York Times*, April 3, 2011, http://www.nytimes.com/2011/04 /04/world/middleeast/04yemen.html?pagewanted=all.

136 **killing more than fifty people:** See "Yemen Unrest: 'Dozens Killed' as Gunmen Target Rally," *BBC*, March 18, 2011, http://www.bbc.co.uk /news/world-middle-east-12783585.

137 **and should be eased out of power:** Kasinof and Sanger.

137 **a leader of the antigovernment youth movement:** Ibid.

137 **Assad of Syria responded:** See Katherine Marsh and Simon Tisdall, "Syrian Troops Shoot Dead Protesters in Day of Turmoil," *Guardian*, April 22, 2011, http://www.theguardian.com/world/2011/apr/22/syria -protests-forces-shoot.

138 **On May 19, 2011, Obama delivered a speech:** See Office of the Press Secretary, "Remarks by the President on the Middle East and North Africa," The White House, May 19, 2011, http://www.whitehouse.gov/the -press-office/2011/05/19/remarks-president-middle-east-and-north -africa.

140 **Anthony Haddad, a twenty-five-year-old student in Beirut:** See "Middle East: Reactions to Obama's Speech," *Los Angeles Times*, May 19, 2011, http://latimesblogs.latimes.com/babylonbeyond/2011/05/reactions -to-obamas-middle-east-speech.html#sthash.KFf0kiEG.dpuf.

141 **a quadrennial strategic review process:** See Bureau of Public Affairs, "Remarks at Town Hall Meeting on the Release of the First Quadrennial Diplomacy and Development Review, 'Leading Through Civilian Power,'" U.S. Department of State, December 15, 2010, http://www .state.gov/secretary/rm/2010/12/152934.htm.

141 **to embrace "economic statecraft":** See Bureau of Public Affairs, "Economic Statecraft," U.S. Department of State, October 14, 2011, http:// www.state.gov/secretary/rm/2011/10/175552.htm.

142 **increasing the department's staff by 25 percent:** See "Foreign Service Midlevel Staffing Gaps Persist Despite Significant Increases in Hiring," Government Accountability Office, June 2012, http://www.gao.gov /assets/600/591595.pdf.

143 **hurled shoes and tomatoes at her car:** See Robert Mackey, "Behind Jeers for Clinton in Egypt, a Conspiracy Theory with U.S. Roots," *The Lede* (blog), *New York Times*, July 16, 2012, http://thelede.blogs.nytimes .com/2012/07/16/egyptians-who-jeered-cLinton-cite-american -conservatives-to-argue-u-s-secretly-supports-islamists.

144 **turned down repeated requests:** See Bureau of Public Affairs, "Accountability Review Board Report," U.S. Department of State, December 19, 2012, http://www.state.gov/documents/organization/202446.pdf.

147 **killed a thousand Brotherhood members:** See Patrick Kingsley, "Tahrir Square Memorial Is Attempt to Co-opt Revolution, Say Egypt Activists," *Guardian*, November 18, 2013, http://www.theguardian.com/world /2013/nov/18/tahrir-square-memorial-co-opt-egypt-revolution?INTC MP=ILCNETTXT3487.

148 **America is not the world's policeman:** See Office of the Press Secretary, "Remarks by President Obama in Address to the United Nations General Assembly," The White House, September 24, 2013, http://www .whitehouse.gov/the-press-office/2013/09/24/remarks-president -obama-address-united-nations-general-assembly.

CHAPTER 9: LITTLE WASHINGTON

150 **thrilled and inspired him:** Interviews with Koltai, July and August 2012.

156 **investor in the sector:** Retrieved from Carlyle Group Web site, August 2012, http://carlyle.com/.

157 **after the 9/11 attacks:** Ibid.

157 **as much as $2 billion each:** Ibid.

159 **$522 million in government contracts:** See *Washington Technology,* "2013 Washington Technology Top 100," November 10, 2013. http:// washingtontechnology.com/toplists/top-100-lists/2013.aspx.

159 **chief innovation officer:** Interview with O'Neill, August 2012.

161 **long-term strategies:** Interview with Chaudhary, August 2012.

BIBLIOGRAPHY

The list below includes articles, books, documents, and reports that I read fully, read partially, or consulted. I am deeply indebted to the courageous work of journalists in the countries I have not visited since 2009: Afghanistan, Pakistan, Libya, and Egypt.

ARTICLES

Abbot, Sebastian. "Pakistan Army Chief Condemns US Drone Attack." Associated Press, March 17, 2011. http://o.seattletimes.nwsource.com/html/nationworld/2014522314_apaspakistan.html.

Abrahams, Fred. "Libya Slogs Toward Democracy." *Daily Beast,* July 24, 2012. http://www.thedailybeast.com/articles/2012/07/24/with-gaddafi-gone-libya-slogs-toward-democracy.html.

Agence France-Presse. "Court Upholds CIA Contractor's Detainee Abuse Conviction." August 11, 2009. http://www.google.com/hostednews/afp/article/ALeqM5gSo6iRtgbNNlDhDyO_VcZEmT45MQ.

Al Arabiya News. "Turkish Soap Star Sparks Divorces in Arab World." June 29, 2008. http://www.alarabiya.net/articles/2008/06/29/52291.html.

Amara, Tarek, and Lin Noueihed. "Tunisian Salafi Islamists Riot over 'Insulting' Art." Reuters, June 12, 2012. http://www.reuters.com/article/2012/06/12/us-tunisia-salafis-clash-idUSBRE85B0XW20120612.

AMEinfo.com. "Beirut Hosts the 2nd New Arab Woman Forum (NAWF)." September 11, 2008. http://www.ameinfo.com/168434.html.

Arango, Tim, and Hwaida Saad. "Turkey's Parliament Backs Military Measures on Syria," *New York Times,* October 4, 2012. http://www.nytimes.com/2012/10/05/world/middleeast/syria.html?pagewanted=1&hp&pagewanted=all.

Arnold, Laurence. "Richard Holbrooke, U.S. Diplomat from Vietnam to Afghanistan, Dies Aged 69." Bloomberg, December 14, 2010. http://www.bloomberg.com/news/2010-12-14/richard-holbrooke-u-s-diplomat-from-vietnam-to-afghanistan-dies-aged-69.html.

Bayrasli, Elmira. "Entrepreneurs Save the World." *World Policy Journal,* Summer 2012. http://www.worldpolicy.org/journal/summer2012/entrepreneurs-save-the-world.

BBC. "Pakistan Anger over Release of CIA Killer Raymond Davis." March 17, 2011. www.bbc.co.uk/news/world-south-asia-12769714.

———. "Yemen Unrest: 'Dozens Killed' as Gunmen Target Rally." March 18, 2011. http://www.bbc.co.uk/news/world-middle-east-12783585.

Ben Bouazza, Bouazza, and Paul Schemm. "Tunisian Radicals Travel to Syria." Associated Press, June 21, 2012. http://bigstory.ap.org/article/tunisian-radicals-travel-syria.

Bilbassy-Charters, Nadia. "Leave It to Turkish Soap Operas to Conquer Hearts and Minds." *Foreign Policy,* April 15, 2010. http://mideast.foreignpolicy.com/posts/2010/04/15/leave_it_to_turkish_soap_operas_to_conquer_hearts_and_minds.

Blair, Dennis C. "Drones Alone Are Not the Answer." *New York Times,* August 14, 2012. http://www.nytimes.com/2011/08/15/opinion/drones-alone-are-not-the-answer.html.

Bohn, Lauren E. "Egypt, as Protests Rage, School Begins." *Daily Beast,* September 15, 2012. http://www.thedailybeast.com/articles/2012/09/15/egypt-as-protests-rage-school-begins.html.

———. "For Egypt's Trapped and Teeming, Revolution Has Barely Begun." CNN, June 7, 2012. http://www.cnn.com/2012/06/07/world/africa/egypt-next-revolution/index.html.

———, and Tim Lister. "The Key to Liberating Egyptians? The Economy." CNN, June 29, 2012. http://articles.cnn.com/2012-06-29/middleeast

/world_meast_egypt-economy_1_muslim-brotherhood-egyptians
-khairat.

Bronner, Ethan, and Michael Slackman. "Saudi Troops Enter Bahrain to
Help Put Down Unrest." *New York Times,* March 14, 2011. http://www
.nytimes.com/2011/03/15/world/middleeast/15bahrain.html?pagewanted
=all.

Buccianti, Alexandra. "Dubbed Turkish Soap Operas Conquering the Arab
World: Social Liberation or Cultural Alienation?" *Arab Media & Society,*
Spring 2010. http://www.arabmediasociety.com/?article=735.

Business Wire. "DynCorp International Inc. to Be Acquired by Cerberus
Capital Management, L.P." April 12, 2010. http://www.businesswire
.com/news/home/20100412006033/en/DynCorp-International
-Acquired-Cerberus-Capital-Management-L.P.

Chandrasekaran, Rajiv. "Cost of War in Afghanistan Will Be Major Factor
in Troop-Reduction Talks." *Washington Post,* May 30, 2011. http://www
.washingtonpost.com/world/national-security/cost-of-war-in
-afghanistan-will-be-major-factor-in-troop-reduction-talks/2011/05/27
/AGR8z2EH_print.html.

———. "U.S. Pursues a New Way to Rebuild in Afghanistan." *Washington
Post,* June 19, 2009. http://www.washingtonpost.com/wp-dyn/content
/article/2009/06/18/AR2009061804135.html.

Chaudhry, Asif. "U.S. Official Guns Down Two Motorcyclists in Lahore."
Dawn, January 28, 2011. http://dawn.com/2011/01/28/us-official-guns
-down-two-motorcyclists-in-lahore/.

Cloud, David S., and Neela Banerjee. "Forces in Bahrain Move Against
Crowd in Square." *Los Angeles Times,* March 16, 2011. http://articles.la
times.com/2011/mar/16/world/la-fg-bahrain-flashpoint-20110316.

Cook, Chris. "Davis Blamed over Gaddafi's Gift to LSE." *Financial Times,*
December 1, 2011. http://www.ft.com/intl/cms/s/0/4971e882-1b63-11e1
-85f8-00144feabdc0.html#axzz250YSEoCM.

Cooper, Helene, Mark Landler, and David E. Sanger. "In U.S. Signals to
Egypt, Obama Straddled a Rift." *New York Times,* February 12, 2011.
http://www.nytimes.com/2011/02/13/world/middleeast/13diplomacy
.html?pagewanted=all.

Corn, David, and Siddhartha Mahanta. "From Libya with Love." *Mother*

Jones, March 3, 2011. http://www.motherjones.com/politics/2011/03 /libya-qaddafi-monitor-group.

Cullather, Nick. "Damming Afghanistan: Modernization in a Buffer State." *Journal of American History* 89, no. 2 (September 2002): 512–37. http:// www.nyu.edu/gsas/dept/icas/Cullather.pdf.

Dawn. "Rare Condemnation by PM, Army Chief: 40 Killed in Drone Attack." March 18, 2011. http://dawn.com/2011/03/18/rare-condemnation -by-pm-army-chief-40-killed-in-drone-attack/.

Dilanian, Ken. "Review: High Salaries for Aid Group CEOs." *USA Today,* September 1, 2009. http://www.usatoday.com/news/world/2009-08-31-us -aid-groups_N.htm#chart.

Eleiba, Ahmed. "Brotherhood's El-Erian Believes Rapprochement with Iran, Hamas in Egypt's Interest." Ahram Online, September 20, 2012. http:// english.ahram.org.eg/NewsContentPrint/1/0/53411/Egypt/0/QA -Brotherhoods-ElErian-believes-rapprochement-wit.aspx.

Ellali, Ahmed. "Several Thousand Salafists Demonstrate for Islamic Law, Attack Dramatists in Tunis." *Tunisia Live,* March 25, 2012. http://www .tunisia-live.net/2012/03/25/several-thousand-salafists-demonstrate-for -islamic-law-attack-dramatists-in-tunis/.

Entous, Adam, Siobhan Gorman, and Julian E. Barnes. "U.S. Tightens Drone Rules." *Wall Street Journal,* November 4, 2011. http://online.wsj .com/article/SB10001424052970204621904577013982672973836.html.

Feinstein, Dianne. "Letters: Sen. Feinstein on Drone Attacks." *Los Angeles Times,* May 17, 2012. http://articles.latimes.com/2012/may/17/opinion /la-le-0517-thursday-feinstein-drones-20120517.

Ferran, Lee. "Raymond Davis, CIA Contractor, Charged with Felony in Parking Lot Skirmish." ABC News, October 4, 2011. http://abcnews.go .com/Blotter/raymond-davis-cia-contractor-charged-parking-lot-fight /story?id=14663216.

Feuillatre, Cecile. "Buoyant Erdogan Sells Turkish Model to Arab Spring." Agence France-Presse, September 14, 2012. http://www.google.com /hostednews/afp/article/ALeqM5iYbCJEmBCnS-3bEXWY9mkd KHxSwA.

Filkins, Dexter. "The Deep State." *New Yorker,* March 12, 2012. http://www .newyorker.com/reporting/2012/03/12/120312fa_fact_filkins.

Finn, Peter. "Obama's Plan to Shutter Guantanamo Faces Hurdles." *Washington Post,* January 22, 2009. http://www.washingtonpost.com/wp-dyn/content/article/2009/01/21/AR2009012101036.html.

Gall, Carlotta, and David Rohde. "Militants Escape Control of Pakistan, Officials Say." *New York Times,* January 15, 2008. www.nytimes.com/2008/01/15/world/asia/15isi.html.

Guardian. "Hosni Mubarak's Speech: Full Text." February 1, 2011. http://www.theguardian.com/world/2011/feb/02/president-hosni-mubarak-egypt-speech.

Hedgpeth, Dana, and Josh Boak. "USAID Suspends District-Based Nonprofit AED from Contracts amid Investigation." *Washington Post,* December 8, 2010.   http://www.washingtonpost.com/wp-dyn/content/article/2010/12/08/AR2010120807665.html.

Kasinof, Laura, and David E. Sanger. "U.S. Shifts to Seek Removal of Yemen's Leader, an Ally." *New York Times,* April 3, 2011. http://www.nytimes.com/2011/04/04/world/middleeast/04yemen.html?pagewanted=all.

Kingsley, Patrick. "Tahrir Square Memorial Is Attempt to Co-opt Revolution, Say Egypt Activists." *Guardian,* November 18, 2013. http://www.theguardian.com/world/2013/nov/18/tahrir-square-memorial-co-opt-egypt-revolution?INTCMP=ILCNETTXT3487.

Landler, Mark. "U.S. Official with Egypt Ties to Meet with Mubarak." *New York Times,* January 31, 2011. http://www.nytimes.com/2011/02/01/world/middleeast/01diplo.html?_r=0.

Lohr, Daniel. "IMF Recommends a Control on Public Expenditures." *Tunisia Live,* August 6, 2012. http://www.tunisia-live.net/2012/08/06/imf-recommends-a-control-on-public-expenditures/.

Los Angeles Times. "Middle East: Reactions to Obama's Speech." May 19, 2011.   http://latimesblogs.latimes.com/babylonbeyond/2011/05/reactions-to-obamas-middle-east-speech.html#sthash.KFf0kiEG.dpuf.

Mackey, Robert. "Behind Jeers for Clinton in Egypt, a Conspiracy Theory with U.S. Roots." *New York Times,* July 16, 2012. http://thelede.blogs.nytimes.com/2012/07/16/egyptians-who-jeered-clinton-cite-american-conservatives-to-argue-u-s-secretly-supports-islamists/.

Magid, Pesha. "Union of Journalists Condemns Proposed Limits on Freedom of Press." *Tunisia Live,* August 8, 2012. http://www.tunisia-live.net

/2012/08/08/union-of-journalists-condemns-proposed-limits-on
-freedom-of-the-press/.

Malek, Abdul. "South African Contractor Held for Killing Afghan Guard."
Reuters, October 3, 2009. http://www.reuters.com/article/2009/10/03/us
-afghanistan-contractor-sb-idUSTRE5921HJ20091003.

Marsh, Katherine, and Simon Tisdall. "Syrian Troops Shoot Dead Protesters
in Day of Turmoil." *Guardian*, April 22, 2011. http://www.theguardian
.com/world/2011/apr/22/syria-protests-forces-shoot.

Matthews, Owen. "The Arab World's 'Dallas.'" *Newsweek*, September 5,
2011. http://www.thedailybeast.com/newsweek/2011/09/04/turkish-soap
-operas-are-sweeping-the-middle-east.html.

Mazzetti, Mark, Ashley Parker, Jane Perlez, and Eric Schmitt. "American
Held in Pakistan Worked with CIA." *New York Times*, February 21, 2011.
http://www.nytimes.com/2011/02/22/world/asia/22pakistan.html?page
wanted=all.

———, and David Rohde. "Amid U.S. Policy Disputes, Qaeda Grows in Pakistan." *New York Times*, June 30, 2008. http://www.nytimes.com/2008
/06/30/washington/30tribal.html.

Miller, Greg, and Karen DeYoung. "U.S., Pakistani Officials at Diplomatic
Odds in Fatal Shooting." *Washington Post*, February 10, 2011. http://
www.washingtonpost.com/wp-dyn/content/article/2011/02/09
/AR2011020906436.html.

Moss, Michael. "Law and Disorder: How Iraq Police Reform Became a Casualty of War." *New York Times*, May 22, 2006. http://www.nytimes.com
/2006/05/22/world/middleeast/22security.html?pagewanted=all.

Moss, Michael, and David Rohde. "Misjudgments Marred U.S. Plans for
Iraqi Police." *New York Times*, May 21, 2006. http://www.nytimes
.com/2006/05/21/world/middleeast/21security.html?pagewanted=all.

Namatalla, Ahmed, and Alaa Shahine. "Egypt Current Account Deficit Wid-
ens as Tourism, FDI Fall." Bloomberg, June 10, 2012. http://www
.bloomberg.com/news/2012-06-10/egypt-current-account-deficit-widens
-as-tourism-fdi-fall-1-.html.

Nawaz, Shuja. "Stilling a Stormy Relationship." *Foreign Policy*, July 12, 2012.
http://afpak.foreignpolicy.com/posts/2012/07/12/stilling_a_stormy
_relationship.

Nebehay, Stephanie. "Syrian Refugees in Turkey Could Top 200,000: U.N." Reuters, August 28, 2012. http://news.yahoo.com/syrians-fleeing-jordan -could-herald-much-larger-influx-093714760.html.

New York Times. "Arab Spring, Fall, and After." February 21, 2012. http:// www.nytimes.com/interactive/2011/11/23/world/middleeast/Arab -Spring-and-Fall.html.

Packer, George. "The Last Mission: Richard Holbrooke's Plan to Avoid the Mistakes of Vietnam in Afghanistan." *New Yorker,* September 28, 2009. http://m.newyorker.com/reporting/2009/09/28/090928fa_fact_ packer?currentPage=all.

Paddock, Barry, Greg B. Smith, and Larry McShane. "Former NYPD Boss Bernard Kerik Released from Federal Prison, Heads Home to N.J." *New York Daily News,* May 28, 2013. http://www.nydailynews.com/new-york /nypd-boss-bernard-kerik-prison-article-1.1356234.

Pilkington, Ed. "The Monitor Group: Gaddafi's PR Firm Used Academics." *Guardian,* March 4, 2011. http://www.guardian.co.uk/world/2011/mar /04/the-monitor-group-gadaffi-pr.

Priest, Dana, and William M. Arkin. "A Hidden World, Growing Beyond Control." *Washington Post,* July 19, 2010. http://projects.washingtonpost .com/top-secret-america/articles/a-hidden-world-growing-beyond -control/.

Richardson, Clem. "Bernie Kerik Copes with Prison Life." *New York Daily News,* June 13, 2012. http://articles.nydailynews.com/2012-06-13 /news/32199756_1_bernie-kerik-hala-matli-bernard-kerik.

Rohde, David. "An Afghan Symbol for Change, Then Failure." *New York Times,* September 5, 2006. www.nytimes.com/2006/09/05/world/asia /05afghan.html.

———. "Can Tunisia Become the Silicon Valley of the Arab World?" *Atlantic,* March 30, 2012. http://www.whitehouse.gov/the-press-office/remarks -president-cairo-university-6-04-09.

———. "Deadly Unrest Leaves a Town Bitter at U.S." *New York Times,* April 20, 2003. http://www.nytimes.com/2003/04/20/world/a-nation-at-war -mosul-deadly-unrest-leaves-a-town-bitter-at-us.html.

———. "Held by the Taliban." *New York Times,* October 17–21, 2009. http:// www.nytimes.com/2009/10/18/world/asia/18hostage.html.

———. "Honoring a Slain Ambassador." Reuters, September 13, 2012. http://blogs.reuters.com/david-rohde/2012/09/13/honoring-a-slain-ambassador/.

———. "How John Kerry Could End Up Outdoing Hillary Clinton." *Atlantic*, November 20, 2013. http://www.theatlantic.com/magazine/archive/2013/12/john-kerry-will-not-be-denied/354688.

———. "The Islamic World's Culture War, Played Out on TV Soap Operas." *Atlantic*, March 9, 2012. http://www.theatlantic.com/international/archive/2012/03/the-islamic-worlds-culture-war-played-out-on-tv-soap-operas/254247/.

———. "The Obama Doctrine: How the President's Drone War Is Backfiring." *Foreign Policy*, March/April 2012. http://www.foreignpolicy.com/articles/2012/02/27/the_obama_doctrine?page=full.

———. "Taliban Raise Poppy Production to a Record Again." *New York Times*, August 26, 2007. http://www.nytimes.com/2007/08/26/world/asia/26heroin.html?pagewanted=all.

———. "Where Islam and Democracy Meet, Uneasily." Reuters, October 21, 2011. http://www.reuters.com/article/2011/10/21/idUS20903515332011 1021.

———, and David E. Sanger, "How a Good War Went Bad in Afghanistan." *New York Times*, August 12, 2007. www.nytimes.com/2007/08/12/world/asia/12afghan.html?pagewanted=all.

———, Carlotta Gall, Eric Schmitt, and David E. Sanger. "U.S. Officials See Waste in Billions Sent to Pakistan." *New York Times*, December 24, 2007. http://www.nytimes.com/2007/12/24/world/asia/24military.html?pagewanted=all.

Rozen, Laura. "Dissent Memo: USAID Official Charges Holbrooke Pakistan AID Plan Flawed." *Politico*, October 12, 2009. http://www.politico.com/blogs/laurarozen/1009/Dissent_Memo_USAID_official_charges_Holbrooke_Pakistan_aid_plan_flawed.html.

Sambidge, Andy. "MBC Expands Soap Opera Shows Despite Mufti Fury." *Arabian Business*, October 21, 2008. http://www.arabianbusiness.com/mbc-expands-soap-opera-shows-despite-mufti-fury-84564.html.

Sanger, David E., and Eric Schmitt. "U.S.-Saudi Tensions Intensify with

Mideast Turmoil." *New York Times*, March 14, 2011. http://www.nytimes
.com/2011/03/15/world/middleeast/15saudi.html?pagewanted=all.

Sappenfield, Mark, and Tracey Samuelson. "Qaddafi UN Speech: Six Highlights—or Lowlights?" *Christian Science Monitor,* September 23, 2009.
http://www.csmonitor.com/USA/Politics/The-Vote/2009/0923/qaddafi
-un-speech-six-highlights-or-lowlights.

Schemm, Paul. "Tunisian Democracy Threatened by Weak Opposition." Associated Press, July 4, 2012. http://bigstory.ap.org/article/tunisian-democracy
-threatened-weak-opposition.

Schmitt, Eric, David Kirkpatrick, and Suliman Ali Zway. "U.S. May Have Put
Mistaken Faith in Libya Site's Security." *New York Times*, October 1, 2012.
http://www.nytimes.com/2012/10/01/world/africa/mistaken-sense-
of-security-cited-before-envoy-to-libya-died.html?pagewanted=all.

Shelton, Tracey. "Libya's Media Has Its Own Revolution." *GlobalPost,*
March 18, 2012. http://www.globalpost.com/dispatch/news/regions/africa
/120301/libya-media-revolution-newspapers-television-radio
-journalism-free-speech.

Taylor, Marisa, and Warren P. Strobel. "U.S. Contractor Accused of Fraud
Still Winning Big Afghan Projects." McClatchy, September 19, 2010.
http://www.mcclatchydc.com/2010/09/19/100690/us-contractor
-accused-of-fraud.html.

Toksabay, Ece, and Ibon Villelabeitia. "Sultan's TV Drama Opens Turkish Divide on Religion." Reuters, February 8, 2011. http://www.reuters.com/article
/2011/02/08/us-turkey-ottoman-drama-idUSTRE7173GA20110208.

Vardi, Nathan. "Wall Street Goes to War." *Forbes,* August 3, 2009. http://
www.forbes.com/forbes/2009/0803/iraq-afghanistan-obama-wall
-street-goes-to-war.html.

Walsh, Declan, and Ewan MacAskill. "A CIA Spy, a Hail of Bullets, Three
Killed and a US-Pakistan Diplomatic Row." *Guardian*, February 20, 2011.
http://www.guardian.co.uk/world/2011/feb/20/cia-agent-lahore
-civilian-deaths.

———, and Ewan MacAskill. "American Who Sparked Diplomatic Crisis
over Lahore Shooting Was CIA Spy." *Guardian,* February 20, 2011. http://
www.guardian.co.uk/world/2011/feb/20/us-raymond-davis-lahore-cia.

Waraich, Omar. "How a U.S. Aid Package Could Threaten Zardari." *Time,* October 8, 2009. http://www.time.com/time/world/article/0,8599,1929 306,00.html.

Washington Technology. "2013 Washington Technology Top 100." November 10, 2013. http://washingtontechnology.com/toplists/top-100-lists/2013 .aspx.

Worth, Robert F. "Arab TV Tests Societies' Limits with Depictions of Sex and Equality." *New York Times,* September 26, 2008. http://www.ny times.com/2008/09/27/world/middleeast/27beirut.html.

Ziezulewicz, Geoff. "With Bahrain Home to 5th Fleet, U.S. Faces Dilemma over Crackdown on Protests." *Stars and Stripes,* February 12, 2012. http:// www.stripes.com/with-bahrain-home-to-5th-fleet-us-faces -dilemma-over-crackdown-on-protests-1.168370.

BOOKS

Chandrasekaran, Rajiv. *Little America: The War Within the War for Afghanistan.* New York: Knopf, 2012.

Chatterjee, Pratap. *Iraq, Inc.: A Profitable Occupation.* New York: Seven Stories Press, 2004.

Chollet, Derek, and Samantha Power. *The Unquiet American: Richard Holbrooke in the World.* New York: PublicAffairs, 2011.

Dobson, William J. *The Dictator's Learning Curve: Inside the Global Battle for Democracy.* New York: Doubleday, 2012.

Dupree, Louis. *Afghanistan.* Oxford: Oxford University Press, 1973.

Dupree, Nancy Hatch. *An Historical Guide to Afghanistan.* Kabul: Afghan Tourist Organization, 1977.

Mann, James. *The Obamians: The Struggle Inside the White House to Redefine American Power.* New York: Viking, 2012.

Osman, Tarek. *Egypt on the Brink: From Nasser to Mubarak.* New Haven: Yale University Press, 2011.

Poullada, Leon B., and D. J. Leila. *The Kingdom of Afghanistan and the United States: 1828–1973.* Omaha and Lincoln, NE: The Center for Afghanistan Studies at the University of Nebraska at Omaha and Dageforde Publishing, 1995.

Rashid, Ahmed. *Descent into Chaos: The United States and the Failure of Nation Building in Pakistan, Afghanistan and Central Asia.* New York: Viking, 2008.

———. *Pakistan on the Brink: The Future of America, Pakistan and Afghanistan.* New York: Viking, 2012.

———. *Taliban: Militant Islam, Oil and Fundamentalism in Central Asia.* New Haven: Yale University Press, 2000.

Sanger, David E. *Confront and Conceal: Obama's Secret Wars and Surprising Use of American Power.* New York: Crown, 2012.

———. *The Inheritance: The World Obama Confronts and the Challenges to American Power.* New York: Crown, 2009.

Shook, Lucy. *Letters from Afghanistan.* Liz Adair, Ruth Lavine, and Terry Gifford, eds. Ferndale, WA: GAL Editing & Publishing, 2002.

Singer, P. W. *Corporate Warriors: The Rise of the Privatized Military Industry.* Ithaca, NY: Cornell University Press, 2003.

Toynbee, Arnold. *Between Oxus and Jumna.* Oxford: Oxford University Press, 1961.

Woodward, Bob. *Bush at War.* New York: Simon & Schuster, 2002.

———. *Obama's Wars.* New York: Simon & Schuster, 2010.

———. *Plan of Attack.* New York: Simon & Schuster, 2004.

———. *State of Denial.* New York: Simon & Schuster, 2006.

———. *The War Within.* New York: Simon & Schuster, 2008.

DOCUMENTS AND REPORTS

Baron, Lloyd. *Sector Analysis: Helmand-Arghandab Valley Region.* Kabul: United States Agency for International Development, 1973.

Belasco, Amy. *The Cost of Iraq, Afghanistan, and Other Global War on Terror Operations Since 9/11.* Washington, DC: Congressional Research Service, 2011. http://www.fas.org/sgp/crs/natsec/RL33110.pdf.

Bureau of Public Affairs. "Accountability Review Board Report." U.S. Department of State, December 19, 2012. http://www.state.gov/documents /organization/202446.pdf

———. "Economic Statecraft." U.S. Department of State, October 14, 2011. http://www.state.gov/secretary/rm/2011/10/175552.htm.

———. "Remarks at Town Hall Meeting on the Release of the First Quadrennial Diplomacy and Development Review, 'Leading Through Civilian

Power.'" U.S. Department of State, December 15, 2010. http://www.state
.gov/secretary/rm/2010/12/152934.htm.

Caudill, Mildred. *Helmand-Arghandab Valley: Yesterday, Today, Tomorrow.*
Lashkar Gah: United States Agency for International Development,
1969.

Clapp-Wincek, Cynthia. *The Helmand Valley Project in Afghanistan.* Washington, DC: United States Agency for International Development, 1983.

Commission on Wartime Contracting. *Transforming Wartime Contracting:
Controlling Costs, Reducing Risks: Final Report to Congress.* Washington,
DC: Government Printing Office, 2011. http://www.wartimecontracting
.gov/docs/CWC_FinalReport-lowres.pdf.

Counterterrorism Strategy Initiative. *The Year of the Drone: An Analysis of
U.S. Drone Strikes in Pakistan, 2004–2012.* Washington, DC: New American Foundation, 2012.

Dobbins, James, et al. *America's Role in Nation-Building: From Germany to
Iraq.* Santa Monica, CA: RAND, 2003.

Government Accountability Office. "Foreign Service Midlevel Staffing Gaps
Persist Despite Significant Increases in Hiring." June 2012. http://www
.gao.gov/assets/600/591595.pdf.

Hamdard, Javid. *The State of Telecommunications and Internet in Afghanistan:
Six Years Later (2006–2012).* Washington, DC: Internews, 2012. http://
www.internews.org/research-publications/state-telecommunications
-and-internet-afghanistan-six-years-later-20062012.

Kaminski, Bartlomiej, and Francis Ng. *Turkey's Evolving Trade Integration
into Pan-European Markets: World Bank Policy Research Working Paper
3908.* Washington, DC: World Bank, 2006.

Moore, Jonathan. *Morality and Foreign Policy.* Hanover, NH: The Dickey
Center, 2007. http://counterterrorism.newamerica.net/drones.

Office of the Press Secretary. "Remarks by President Obama and Prime Minister Stephen Harper of Canada in Joint Press Availability." Washington,
DC: The White House, February 4, 2011. http://www.whitehouse.gov/the
-press-office/2011/02/04/remarks-president-obama-and-prime-minister
-stephen-harper-canada-joint-p.

———. "Remarks by President Obama in Address to the United Nations
General Assembly." Washington, DC: The White House, September 24,

2013. http://www.whitehouse.gov/the-press-office/2013/09/24/remarks-president-obama-address-united-nations-general-assembly.

———. "Remarks by the President on a New Beginning." Washington, DC: The White House, 2009. http://www.whitehouse.gov/the-press-office/remarks-president-cairo-university-6-04-09.

———. "Remarks by the President on the Middle East and North Africa." Washington, DC: The White House, May 19, 2011. http://www.whitehouse.gov/the-press-office/2011/05/19/remarks-president-middle-east-and-north-africa.

Office of Public Affairs. "Husband and Wife Co-owners of Subcontracting Company Plead Guilty to Contract Fraud Related to Afghanistan Rebuilding." Washington, DC: Department of Justice, 2009. http://www.justice.gov/opa/pr/2009/September/09-crm-943.html.

———. "Washington, D.C.–Based Academy for Educational Development Pays More Than $5 Million to Settle False Claims Act Allegations." Washington, DC: Department of Justice, 2011. http://www.justice.gov/usao/dc/news/2011/jun/11-278.pdf.

Office of the Special Inspector General for Afghanistan Reconstruction. *Afghanistan's National Solidarity Program Has Reached Thousands of Afghan Communities, but Faces Challenges That Could Limit Outcomes.* Washington, DC: Government Printing Office. 2011. http://www.sigar.mil/pdf/audits/2011-03-22audit-11-08.pdf.

Pew Global Attitudes Project. *Egyptians Remain Optimistic, Embrace Democracy and Religion in Political Life.* Washington, DC: Pew Research Center, 2012. http://www.pewglobal.org/2012/05/08/chapter-5-views-of-the-united-states-and-israel/.

———. *Most Muslims Want Democracy, Personal Freedoms, and Islam in Political Life.* Washington, DC: Pew Research Center, 2012. http://www.pewglobal.org/2012/07/10/chapter-8-tunisias-relationship-with-the-u-s/.

———. *Pakistani Public Opinion Ever More Critical of U.S.* Washington, DC: Pew Research Center, 2012. http://www.pewglobal.org/2012/06/27/pakistani-public-opinion-ever-more-critical-of-u-s/.

Phillips, Macon. "President Barack Obama's Inaugural Address." Washington, DC: The White House Blog, 2009. http://www.whitehouse.gov/blog/inaugural-address.

BIBLIOGRAPHY

Sharp, Jeremy M. *Egypt: Transition Under Military Rule*. Washington, DC: Congressional Research Service, June 21, 2012, 14–24. http://fpc.state .gov/documents/organization/194799.pdf.

United States Agency for International Development. *Afghanistan Mortality Survey: 2010 Health Study Shows Significant Gains in Afghan Maternal and Child Health*. Washington, DC: Government Printing Office, 2012. http://transition.usaid.gov/locations/afghanistanpakistan/countries /afghanistan/ams2010.html.

World Factbook. *Country Comparison: GDP—Real Growth Rate 2012*. Langley, VA: Central Intelligence Agency, 2012. https://www.cia.gov/library/publica tions/the-world-factbook/rankorder/2003rank.html?countryName=Turkey &countryCode=tu&regionCode=mde&rank=15#tu.

INDEX

CREDITS

Portions of this book first appeared as "The Last Mission" in *The Unquiet American: Richard Holbrooke in the World*, Derek Chollet and Samantha Power, editors (Public Affairs, 2011), and "The Obama Doctrine: How the President's Drone War Is Backfiring," *Foreign Policy*, issue of February 27, 2012.

Grateful acknowledgment is made for permission to reprint the following works by David Rohde (or excerpts therefrom):

The New York Times: "In Newly Occupied Mosul, U.S. Colonel Faces 1.7 Million Added Responsibilities," issue of April 13, 2003; "Misjudgments Marred U.S. Plans for Iraqi Police" (by Michael Moss and David Rohde), May 21, 2006; "An Afghan Symbol for Change, Then Failure," September 5, 2006; "Taliban Raise Poppy Production to a Record Again," August 26, 2007; and "Personal Diplomacy," December 26, 2010. © 2003, 2006, 2007, 2010 The New York Times. All rights reserved. Used by permission and protected by the copyright laws of the United States. The printing, copying, redistribution, or retransmission of this content without express written permission is prohibited.

Reuters: "Where Islam and Democracy Meet, Uneasily," issue of October 21, 2011; "Talk for Now in Syria but Prepare to Arm," February 24, 2012; "Inside Islam's Culture War," March 8, 2012; "The Arab World's Silicon Valley?" March 30, 2012; "The Islamist Spring," April 5, 2012; "Little America: An Afghan town, an American Dream and the Folly of For-Profit War," June 1, 2012; "Honoring a Slain Ambassador," September 13, 2012; "Republicans Betray their Foreign Policy Tradition," September 19, 2012; "A Hidden Cause of Benghazi Tragedy," November 16, 2012; and "Morsi's Folly," November 23, 2012. Reprinted by arrangement with Reuters.

AVAILABLE FROM PENGUIN

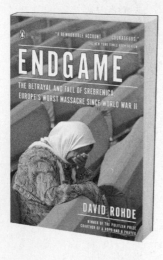

Endgame
The Betrayal and Fall of Srebrenica, Europe's Worst Massacre Since World War II

In 1996, at the height of the Bosnian wars, David Rohde uncovered a horrifying story that became an enduring symbol of the genocidal nature of that conflict, earning him his first Pulitzer Prize. *Endgame* is the comprehensive account of the tragic fall and massacre of Srebrenica. This is an unforgettable work of history about an atrocity with reverberations even today.

ISBN 978-0-14-312031-5

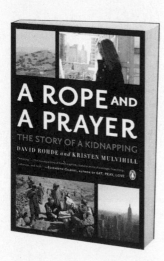

A Rope and a Prayer
The Story of a Kidnapping
Written with Kristen Mulvihill

In November 2008, David Rohde, a Pulitzer Prize-winning correspondent for *The New York Times*, was kidnapped by the Taliban and held captive for seven months in Pakistan. Meanwhile in New York, his wife Kristin Mulvihill, struggled to navigate a labyrinth of conflicting agendas, misinformation, and lies. Part memoir, part work of journalism, Rohde and Mulvihill craft a compelling story of terror, faith, resilience, and love.

ISBN 978-0-14-312005-6

PENGUIN BOOKS